NEW DIRECTIONS FOR INSTITUTIONAL RESEARCH

J. Fredericks Volkwein, *State University of New York at Albany*
EDITOR-IN-CHIEF

Inter-Institutional Data Exchange: When to Do It, What to Look for, and How to Make It Work

James F. Trainer
Franklin and Marshall College

EDITOR

Number 89, Spring 1996

JOSSEY-BASS PUBLISHERS
San Francisco

INTER-INSTITUTIONAL DATA EXCHANGE: WHEN TO DO IT, WHAT TO LOOK FOR, AND HOW TO MAKE IT WORK
James F. Trainer (ed.)
New Directions for Institutional Research, no. 89
Volume XVIII, Number 1
J. Fredericks Volkwein, Editor-in-Chief

Copyright © 1996 by Jossey-Bass Inc., Publishers, 350 Sansome Street, San Francisco, CA 94104-1342.

All rights reserved. No part of this publication may be reproduced, stored in a retrieval system, or transmitted, in any form or by any means, electronic, mechanical, photocopying, recording, or otherwise, without the prior written permission of the publisher.

Microfilm copies of issues and articles are available in 16mm and 35mm, as well as microfiche in 105mm, through University Microfilms Inc., 300 North Zeeb Road, Ann Arbor, Michigan 48106-1346.

LC 85-645339   ISSN 0271-0579   ISBN 0-7879-9874-5

NEW DIRECTIONS FOR INSTITUTIONAL RESEARCH is part of The Jossey-Bass Higher and Adult Education Series and is published quarterly by Jossey-Bass Inc., Publishers, 350 Sansome Street, San Francisco, California 94104-1342 (publication number USPS 098-830). Second-class postage paid at San Francisco, California, and at additional mailing offices. POSTMASTER: Send address changes to New Directions for Institutional Research, Jossey-Bass Inc., Publishers, 350 Sansome Street, San Francisco, California 94104-1342.

SUBSCRIPTIONS for 1996 cost $50.00 for individuals and $72.00 for institutions, agencies, and libraries.

EDITORIAL CORRESPONDENCE should be sent to J. Fredericks Volkwein, Institutional Research, Administration 241, State University of New York at Albany, Albany, NY 12222.

Photograph of the library by Michael Graves at San Juan Capistrano by Chad Slattery © 1984. All rights reserved.

Manufactured in the United States of America on Lyons Falls Pathfinder Tradebook. This paper is acid-free and 100 percent totally chlorine-free.

THE ASSOCIATION FOR INSTITUTIONAL RESEARCH was created in 1966 to benefit, assist, and advance research leading to improved understanding, planning, and operation of institutions of higher education. Publication policy is set by its Publications Board.

PUBLICATIONS BOARD

Larry G. Jones (Chair)　　University of Georgia
Ansly A. Abraham　　Southern Regional Education Board
Susan H. Frost　　Emory University
Gary R. Hanson　　University of Texas, Austin
Mary Ann Heverly　　Delaware County Community College
Michael W. Matier　　Cornell University

EX-OFFICIO MEMBERS OF THE PUBLICATIONS BOARD

Jean J. Endo　　University of Colorado, Boulder
John A. Lucas　　William Rainey Harper College
Larry W. Nelson　　Pacific Lutheran University
John C. Smart　　University of Illinois–Chicago
Patrick T. Terenzini　　The Pennsylvania State University

For information about the Association for Institutional Research, write to the following address:

AIR Executive Office
314 Stone Building
Florida State University
Tallahassee, FL 32306-3038

(904) 644-4470

Contents

EDITOR'S NOTES 1
James F. Trainer

1. To Share and Share Alike: The Basic Ground Rules 5
for Inter-Institutional Data Sharing
James F. Trainer
Successful inter-institutional data-sharing activities depend on the development of and adherence to a set of commonly shared ground rules.

2. Benefits and Potential Problems Associated with Effective 15
Data-Sharing Consortia
Mary M. Sapp
The benefits and potential problems associated with data sharing are examined from both an institutional perspective and the perspective of the individual institutional researcher.

3. Data-Sharing Models 29
Susan M. Shaman, Daniel Shapiro
Data-sharing models are defined by examining the organization and activities of existing data-sharing groups across eleven different dimensions.

4. Creating a Cost-Effective Data Exchange 41
E. Raymond Hackett
The costs of participating in a data exchange are examined both as they relate to the actual financial costs of engaging in such an activity and the opportunity costs associated with making an uninformed decision.

5. Data Sharing and Keeping Pace with Changing Technologies 53
James C. Fergerson
As computing technologies have continued to evolve, data-sharing activities have been greatly enhanced.

6. Coming Aboard: Making the Decision to Join a Data-Sharing 71
Organization
James F. Trainer
Numerous factors including data availability, financial costs, personnel time, and technological resources should be considered before making a decision to engage in inter-institutional data sharing.

Appendix A: A Computer and Network Resource Guide 79
to Support Data Sharing
James C. Fergerson

Appendix B: Data-Sharing Organizations, Resources, 91
and Opportunities
James F. Trainer

INDEX 105

Editor's Notes

For many years, colleges and universities have participated in various inter-institutional cooperative efforts in numerous arenas. We are all familiar with examples of such activities—interlibrary loans, student and faculty exchanges, cross-course listings, and purchasing cooperatives—to name but a few. Recently, in addition to these more traditional activities, the number of inter-institutional data-sharing opportunities and activities has been on the rise. Once a luxury enjoyed only by large, wealthy, and well-staffed research universities, data exchanges are now available to nearly every type of institution. More and more institutions find themselves either participating in or wishing to become members of various data-sharing partnerships. This recent increase in data-sharing activities has been spawned in part by challenging economic times and calls for increased institutional accountability.

Over the past few years, legislators, trustees, central administrators, students, and the public have increased their scrutiny of institutions and have called for greater institutional effectiveness and public accountability. Colleges and universities have been pushed to enhance institutional quality and to improve institutional efficiency. In short, they have been challenged to do more with less. As a result, campus and system administrators find themselves confronting cost-saving issues on practically a daily basis. At the heart of such issues often lies a deceptively simple question, namely, What economies can we capture to help make our institution(s) both more efficient and effective? Responding to such a question is not always easy. Administrators must decide what actions can be taken to make their institutions more efficient without compromising their institutional strengths. Such pressures are forcing administrators toward a greater emphasis on the use of comparative data to inform institutional decision making. In turn, institutional leaders are on a constant search for those data industry standards that can be employed to compare their own performance in certain areas with that of their peer institutions. Fortunately, more of these data are available today than ever before.

In this volume, the chapter authors highlight the benefits and risks associated with participating in inter-institutional data exchanges and describe the various types of exchanges that are available. They outline data-sharing activities, from rather simple institution-to-institution exchanges to more complex multi-level, multi-institution data-sharing consortia. They describe the mechanics of data exchange from rudimentary copying of paper surveys and reports to more technologically advanced electronic data submission and retrieval. They indicate how data exchanges can serve to enhance the planning processes both on individual campuses and within larger systems. Conversely, they identify potential pitfalls related to openly sharing data with other institutions.

Finally, they provide a blueprint for deciding whether it is in an institution's best interest to engage in this type of activity.

In Chapter One, I outline some of the basic concepts and precepts of data-sharing activities. I review the ground rules, so to speak, of both basic and more complex data exchanges. Through this background material, the reader should gain an appreciation for the decisions involved in deciding whether to participate in inter-institutional data sharing.

In Chapter Two, Mary Sapp discusses the benefits and potential problems associated with effective data-sharing consortia. She examines the benefits and potential problems related to data sharing from an overall institutional perspective as well as from the perspective of the individual staff member who might be responsible for coordinating an institution's participation in an exchange activity. Realizing that engaging in any activity has both benefits and potential liabilities, Sapp argues that institutions need to conduct a cost-benefits analysis at multiple levels prior to arriving at a decision to join a data-sharing consortium.

In Chapter Three, Susan Shaman and Dan Shapiro develop a typology of various data-sharing models. They consider a total of eleven dimensions in arriving at this typology. These dimensions include factors such as the organizational purpose and structure of the data-sharing group, the scope and regularity of surveys conducted by the group, the medium used for the submission of data and subsequent release of reports, and the criteria for institutional participation. After developing their typology, the authors show how various existing data-sharing organizations fit into this framework.

In Chapter Four, Raymond Hackett examines the costs of establishing a data-sharing exchange. He reviews these costs both in terms of actual financial outlays and in terms of the other resources that must be committed to developing such an exchange. Ultimately, he argues that even the combination of financial and resource costs involved in creating such a data-sharing group is minimal when compared to the potential liabilities that may exist in making decisions without access to good comparative information.

Jim Fergerson uses Chapter Five to discuss the use of technology in data-sharing activities. Drawing on the experience of the Higher Education Data Sharing Consortium (HEDS), he traces the evolution of technology and its impact on the development of a data-sharing organization. Fergerson argues that data sharers must realize that technology is only a means to an end, and that participants must keep their eye on the main objective of the activity rather than becoming either enamored with or frustrated by the technology at hand. In the end, however, he suggests that the future of data sharing is indeed bright, given the opportunities that technological advances should afford us in this area.

In the final chapter, I draw upon all these contributions to develop a decision tree to help institutions and individuals decide whether they want to engage in data sharing, and, if so, what type of activity they might want to pursue. In doing so, I pose a series of questions that potential data-sharing participants will want to address in reaching a decision regarding their potential involvement in exchanging data. These questions include such issues as benefits and liabilities, financial costs, the types of information being sought by institutions, and the technologies needed for various levels of exchange. I also provide insight into the types of products that can result from effective data exchange.

In addition to the traditional chapters offered in this issue, the volume also contains two resource appendices for readers who wish to explore data exchanges further. The first, developed by Jim Fergerson, highlights a host of technological resources available to facilitate and foster data sharing. These include various Internet and World Wide Web addresses and resources, software titles, and information on general computing references and tutorials. The second appendix lists data-sharing organizations, opportunities, and resources, and provides a brief description for each listing.

The opportunities for involvement in data-sharing activities are burgeoning. The authors and editors hope that this volume will prove to be a useful tool in helping institutional researchers and planners to take full advantage of this cresting wave. The discussion opened by this volume will be carried on electronically for one year following publication, via a LISTSERV mailing list named NDIRcoop, dedicated to the topic *cooperative data sharing for institutional research*. To participate in this discussion, send an e-mail message to: listserv@mitvma.mit.edu. The text of your message should consist of one line ending with your name: subscribe ndircoop firstname lastname.

You will receive confirmation from the list server. Once you have subscribed to the list, e-mail that you send to NDIRcoop@mitvma.mit.edu will be distributed to everyone else who is subscribed to this list. Anything sent to the list by any other subscriber will be sent to you. Should you wish to cancel your subscription, send e-mail to: listserv@mitvma.mit.edu with the text: unsubscribe NDIRcoop.

Do not send cancellation requests to NDIRcoop, because this will inflict them on all subscribers to the list! If you have any difficulty subscribing or canceling your subscription, send a notification of your problem to litten@mit.edu.

James F. Trainer
Editor

JAMES F. TRAINER *is the director of the Higher Education Data Sharing Consortium located on the campus of Franklin and Marshall College in Lancaster, Pennsylvania. He is a member of the Association for Institutional Research's Higher Education Data Policy Committee and the National Association of Independent Colleges and Universities' Commission on Policy Analysis.*

This chapter proposes a set of general policies or ground rules that data exchanges may want to consider in establishing and guiding their activities.

To Share and Share Alike: The Basic Ground Rules for Inter-Institutional Data Sharing

James F. Trainer

Colleges and universities, and the individual administrators, faculty, and staff members associated with them, belong to many organizations and participate in numerous inter-institutional arrangements. The *1996 Higher Education Directory,* for instance, contains information on 303 Higher Education Associations and another 106 Consortia of Institutions of Higher Education, excluding statewide agencies of Higher Education (Higher Education Publications, 1995). Undoubtedly, many other groups exist beyond these, because presumably the listings in the *Higher Education Directory* are restricted to groups that are formally organized. Regardless of whether they are formally organized or not, however, associations and consortia exist to meet the collective needs of their institutional members. We are all familiar with many of these groups. Among the organizations most familiar to us are the disciplinary societies to which individual faculty members belong and the Washington, D.C.-based associations that represent the political interests of institutions. However, the *Higher Education Directory* listings also include organizations focused on student and faculty exchanges, cross-course registration arrangements, interlibrary loans, and purchasing cooperatives, to name but a few examples.

These activities are not a recent phenomenon. Contemporary inter-institutional efforts are extensions of a cooperative practice that began as early as 1925 with the collaboration of the Claremont Colleges and rapidly increased in momentum in the early 1960s as a result of the discussions aimed to foster collaboration among higher education institutions (Patterson, 1974). (See Patterson's work for a typology of consortial arrangements and profiles of nearly ninety consortial efforts that existed as of 1974.)

Although the preceding discussion highlights the fact that higher education groups have been coming together for quite some time and for a variety of reasons, increasingly the consortia organized today seek to help their member institutions save money in tight budgetary times (Nicklin, 1994). One way institutions can economize is through participation in formally organized inter-institutional data exchanges.

Recent trends in higher education suggest that the need for comparative data will only increase. For instance, borrowing from business, trustees have called for institutions to use benchmarking as a means to examine their processes and outcomes relative to the best practices in the industry. Likewise, legislators and the public have called for increased accountability and better evidence of institutional outcomes. Regional accrediting agencies have insisted on the establishment of outcomes assessment programs and the production of performance indicators (Borden & Banta, 1994). In addition, consumers—potential students and their parents—encouraged in part by a penchant for ratings and rankings fostered by publications such as *U.S. News & World Report* and *Money Magazine* have driven institutional officials to be more aware than ever about where their institutions stand relative to others.

The factors highlighted above suggest that comparative data will continue to be a much-sought-after commodity. In turn, institutional researchers are placing a greater emphasis on data-sharing activities. This increased focus on data sharing is borne out in part by the fact that no less than fourteen sessions and seven special interest group meetings at the Association for Institutional Research's 35th Annual Forum in Boston in 1995 centered on some form of data-exchange activity.

Before turning our attention exclusively to organized data exchanges, however, it may be helpful to think about the common elements that the various types of groups mentioned above share, regardless of their function, in order to see how data exchanges fit into a lexicon of higher education with which we are already familiar. We can then better examine the specific details of data-sharing organizations that set them apart from other associations and consortia.

First and foremost, the various types of associations and consortia previously cited exist to address a need common to their members, and their success in addressing this need depends on the willingness of their members to participate in the group's activities. Second, the groups described are voluntary in nature; individuals and institutions belong to them of their own choosing. Third, group members share in the operating costs and governance of the organizations to which they belong. Finally, in order for these cooperative groups to function effectively, their members must adhere to the principles or rules established to guide member behavior.

In many ways, athletic conferences may serve as a prototype for inter-institutional cooperative arrangements. Institutions voluntarily belong to athletic conferences to provide, at the very least, extracurricular activities for students and social events for campus communities. Member institutions split conference operating expenses and, in some cases, also share in revenues. Institutions obviously participate in their conference's activities, and, not as obviously, share the governing responsibilities for their conference with their fellow conference members. Ultimately, the overall success of any conference depends on the willingness of its member schools to abide by the rules established to guide their behavior as conference members. Otherwise, a conference may fold for lack of a shared vision and a commitment to cooperation.

Data exchanges are not unlike athletic conferences and other inter-institutional cooperative ventures. For reasons that will be highlighted in this chapter, however, data exchanges can take on a complexity beyond that of other organizations. At the very least, data exchanges must address issues related to how the data to be shared will be collected, analyzed, stored, and distributed, as well as to who will be responsible for these tasks. Exchange organizers also may need to decide what techniques will be used to ensure the integrity of the collected data and how the interests of the institutions that have submitted them will be protected. In turn, organizers should determine what agreements, if any, will be established and followed regarding the use of shared data.

The remainder of this chapter examines these complexities, in addition to the elements common to all voluntary higher education organizations. The chapter outlines a set of general policies, or ground rules, that data exchanges may want to consider in establishing and guiding their activities. Although drawn for the most part from the author's experience with the Higher Education Data Sharing Consortium (HEDS), these ground rules should prove transferable to other data-sharing organizations and situations.

Data Exchange Ground Rules

Just as colleges and universities participate in many cooperative ventures, they also collect, analyze, and distribute large amounts of data concerning the operation of their individual institutions. Institutional leaders and decision makers use data to monitor the general condition of their institutions, to guide their decision-making processes, to measure their success in achieving certain strategic initiatives, and to report to governing bodies and internal and external constituencies. When data from comparable institutions are available, decision makers may also use data to measure the condition of their own institutions relative to that of others.

To accomplish this latter task, decision makers must have data from other institutions available to them. Inter-institutional data exchanges address this need. In order to ensure that this common need is met for all participants, however, it is important that data exchanges establish and abide by a set of ground rules, or operating principles. (See Dunn, 1987 and Chapter Four in this volume for additional information on establishing data exchanges.)

Data Exchanges Are Voluntary, Participatory Organizations. By their very nature, the inter-institutional data exchanges described in this volume are voluntary and participatory. Exchange organizers, therefore, must realize that participation in their activities, no matter how well designed and structured, will vary by institution and research topic. Absent mandates from external agencies, institutions will decide on their own accord whether to engage in a given data exchange, and once having decided to do so, will set their own level and duration of participation. Each exchange member will decide its own level of participation, with the overall participation levels for various projects varying by topic. Quite simply, exchange members will vary in the level of their interest in various research endeavors. A burning issue on one campus may be of little importance at another institution; thus one institution may decide to participate in an exchange on a given topic, whereas another institution may opt out of the same endeavor. There are steps, however, that exchange organizers can follow to enhance participation in their efforts.

Data exchanges should define their memberships carefully. Although institutions may desire to join a data-sharing group, not all groups are appropriate for all institutions. Data from certain colleges and universities will not always prove useful to others. Thus, it is helpful for organizations to give some thought to how their membership is to be defined and what criteria will be used in selecting appropriate members. Often the criteria employed in selecting institutions for membership in a data exchange (whether formal or informal) are similar to the standards that define various groups to which potential data-sharing institutions may already belong. Existing consortia and groups, such as cross-course registration and purchasing arrangements, athletic conferences, and mission-specific organizations may serve as the basis for defining membership in a data-sharing group. In addition, data exchanges might want to consider items such as institutional control (public versus private), type (not-for-profit versus proprietary), mission (two-year only, four-year, religious, research university), enrollment size, regional proximity, and admissions selectivity when choosing criteria to guide the selection of institutions for their membership.

Once formed, data-sharing groups may serve in a sense as de facto peer groups for individual institutional participants. In larger data exchanges, however, it is sometimes necessary for members to pare the overall membership data base down to a smaller size in order to include only data from similar schools. Such is the case in the HEDS Consortium. HEDS, however, is not in the business of identifying peer groups. We believe that each college or university should choose the comparison group appropriate for the purpose of a specific study. In turn, HEDS supplies the complete data base for a given study to all the members that have submitted data for that particular study. Individual institutions then select from that complete data set the specific information they wish to use to meet their needs.

The key to success for a data exchange is the cooperation of its members. No requirements can exist to force members to participate or remain in an exchange once they join. Thus, the organization may need to provide incentives, or at least eliminate disincentives, in order to encourage the participation of as many members as possible in as many of the group's activities as possible. On the surface, such a remark on the need for cooperation in the operation of a self-selecting, voluntary organization may seem silly. However, it is helpful to recognize up front that not every member of an organization will elect to take full advantage of the opportunities afforded it by virtue of membership in that group. It is no different in a data exchange.

Consistent participation in a data exchange may vary depending on the overall scope of the exchange. It stands to reason that one should expect an institution that joins a consortium with a singular focus, such as the Consortium for Student Retention Data Exchange (CSRDE), to participate fully in that group's limited but important activity. It might be unreasonable, however, to expect organizations that have a broader focus and conduct a wider range of studies, such as the Association of American Universities Data Exchange (AAUDE) or HEDS, to have all of their members participate in each of their activities. Members of these latter groups tend to pick and choose the studies in which they will participate. Nonetheless, it is helpful for organizations to find mechanisms to encourage the highest and most consistent levels of participation possible.

The key to encouraging high participation levels in an exchange's activities is adhering to a strict policy limiting access to data from a project to those institutions that have supplied the requisite data themselves. Unfortunately, these decisions are not always clear-cut, especially in cases where individual studies have multiple parts. For instance, a finance study may ask for information on expenditures, revenues, endowment portfolios, physical plant assets, and institutional indebtedness, yet some institutions may choose to submit only a portion of this information. In this case, it may be necessary to look at the given study to determine where the line will be drawn in providing or denying an institution access to any or all of the data from the study if the institution itself has not supplied all of the data requested in the study.

Make participation in the exchange as easy as possible. Because they require some time and effort on the part of participants, exchanges should be careful not to overburden their member institutions. Whenever feasible, exchange activity should build upon work the institutions are already doing. There is no need to reinvent the wheel with every study. Exchanges should share existing national or professional organization surveys whenever possible, developing their own instruments only when absolutely necessary. Rather than creating new studies from whole cloth, exchanges should see if they can build upon an existing survey by simply adding supplemental or clarifying questions to it. HEDS, for instance, supplements the American Association of University Professors (AAUP) Annual Faculty Compensation Survey by asking members to submit a copy of this survey to HEDS along with the answers to a few extremely short questions about certain benefit packages and the salaries for adjunct and new starting assistant professors.

An exchange should deliver a consistent, high quality product or service in a timely fashion and in a format that is useful to its members. Data files of poor quality are generally of little use. Likewise, data files delivered to member campuses beyond the time when they could have been helpful in informing a decision-making process are useless. Data files that require large amounts of work in order for them to be useful may be shelved indefinitely. Thus, issues of data quality, timeliness, and usefulness are central to the success of the data exchange. Useful data are the drawing card for any effective data-sharing organization.

Defining the Scope of the Organization. It is important that data exchanges define the scope of their activity given that any number of areas are open for data sharing. Akin to the previous discussion of a common need generally bringing institutions together and causing the creation of an organization, defining the appropriate terrain for a data exchange will help to determine the exchange's ultimate success. The bottom line is that the exchange must meet the needs of its members.

The scope of individual data exchanges run the gamut from focused, singular issue exchanges (like the CSRDE) to the holistic, multidimensional exchanges like the AAUDE, College Information Systems Association (CISA), and HEDS. Most exchanges fall somewhere in between. Indeed, many exchanges are actually offshoots of organizations drawn together to serve a broader purpose (for example, the Association of American Universities in the case of the AAUDE or the Commission of Independent Colleges and Universities of Pennsylvania in the case of the Pennsylvania Independent College and University Research Center). In fact, it is likely that very few data exchanges would exist without the support of a larger, broader operation.

The links that draw and hold exchanges together are often related to mission or regional affiliation. In turn, the reason and manner in which exchanges are initially created will often help define their scope. This is especially true for organizations that have their roots in other entities. It is clear, for instance, that the work of the Coalition for Christian Colleges and Universities (CCCU) is defined by a desire to promote the advancement of like-minded Christian institutions. Thus, both the membership and scope of the CCCU are well defined.

It is also true, however, that stand-alone data exchanges and their activities are influenced by the groups' initial undertakings. The Consortium on Financing Higher Education (COFHE), for example, initially came together, as its name implies, as part of a study on institutional finance, and even though it serves a broader mission today, much of its energies are still focused on annual surveys of admissions and admissions costs, tuition and fees, financial aid, and on cost studies in other areas.

Exchanges must clearly identify the types of data that will be shared. The best way to do this is to begin sharing data that institutions already have on hand (information that they collect and maintain anyway), and to focus attention on those data that can be most useful in informing the decision-making process at member institutions. Whether organizations came together solely as data-exchange operations or as offshoots of other organizations is inconsequential to the need to focus organizational energies on sharing the data most appropriate to the organization's mission.

Cost, Resource, and Governance Issues. Depending on their size, scope, operating procedures, and level of complexity, data-sharing organizations vary across a number of cost, resource, and governance issues. For instance, some data exchanges may involve little or no financial expense to their members, but other exchanges may levy a membership fee on institutions or collect fees on a per-study basis to support their operations. Likewise, some organizations may require few if any resources beyond the goodwill and volunteer time of their members to run their activities, whereas other organizations may have independent, self-standing offices and staffs. Finally, some groups may exist and be governed in an entirely ad hoc fashion, whereas others may be fully incorporated with their own boards of directors.

Any data-sharing model can be effective as long as it meets the needs of its members. In some cases, simply copying and sharing existing forms, such as the IPEDS (Integrated Postsecondary Education Data System) series, may be sufficient to meet the needs of a loosely formed group. In other cases, electronic data submission and retrieval, extensive data cleaning and manipulation, and detailed analyses or polished reports may be the norm. Obviously, the former case requires few if any resources, whereas the latter case is resource intensive. (See Chapter Three for additional information on various data-sharing models.)

When data-sharing groups are initially formed, the decisions that the founding institutions make about the scope, nature, and purpose of the data they plan to share will in many ways drive future decisions about how those groups will be financed, what resources will be required to let them function effectively, and how they will be governed into the future. Some groups will deliberately decide to keep things as simple as possible; others will build elaborate organizational structures. These decisions will depend largely on each group's initial goals. Thus, if an exchange emerges to address a single issue in an ad hoc fashion without the immediate or anticipated support of an existing organization, it is likely that it will begin simply and remain that way. On the other hand, if a group is spawned as an offshoot of an existing organization, such as a mission-specific or regional association, it is likely to mirror the structure and complexity of the organization from whence it originates. Likewise, an organization formed with ambitious goals from the outset is likely to create a complex structure in order to sustain itself. The important thing is that the organization and its goals fit its membership and their desires. Member institutions will generally create and continue organizations that best meet their needs; data exchanges are no exception.

Data Use Issues. Once a decision has been reached that a group of institutions will begin to share data cooperatively, a number of additional and equally important decisions must be made regarding how data sharing will take place and how the interests of both the individual institutional members and the larger group will be protected. These represent extremely important issues that should be addressed in advance of any actual exchange of data.

Exchanges must first determine how decisions affecting the group will be made. In general, these decisions are best made in a democratic way, each institution with a vested interest in the decision having a say in the decision, either directly or through a representative form of governance. In the HEDS Consortium, for instance, most decisions are made by a duly-elected board of directors, but certain decisions are reserved for the membership as a whole at its annual meeting. The functioning of HEDS in this regard is not unlike that of a publicly-held corporation.

Each institution should formally identify an individual who will speak on its behalf. This may not be the person who will have the most regular ongoing contact with the consortium. The latter requires an individual who will have the time and support needed to participate fully in the data-sharing activities of the consortium; the former requires someone with decision-making authority. It is not unusual for an institution to have a vice-president serve as its official representative to the exchange and a director or manager serve as the ongoing, regular contact with the group.

Institutions' official representatives to the group must be able to guarantee that their institutions will abide by the policies established to direct the activities of the exchange. These policies may include ensuring that appropriate levels of confidentiality will be maintained for the data received through the exchange, that the data will not be released to third parties, that the data will be used only for internal planning purposes and will not be released for external publication, and that appropriate permission will be sought if the data are to be used for reasons other than institutional planning, such as for a conference presentation.

Institutions are only eligible to receive data when they themselves have shared data. Institutions must abide by a "fair play" rule, which provides that an institution is entitled to receive information from other members only in those areas and for those years for which it has provided comparable information.

Institutions should adhere to a basic "do no harm" rule in determining whether a potential use of the data on their campuses is within the overall spirit of the organization. Institutional participants must realize that other institutions have a proprietary interest in the data they make available and that there is a shared risk in exchanging data. Institutions should always make decisions about the appropriate use of data as though the shoe was on the other foot, so to speak, and they themselves had provided the information.

Conclusion

The success of any data-sharing group, much like any other cooperative arrangement, will depend on the willing and full participation of all of its members. Individual institutional participation in the group can be fostered by having a well-defined and comparable membership that is meaningful to the members, by establishing a clear set of organizational objectives and data to be shared, by delivering a high quality timely product with a limited burden on the members themselves, and by maintaining and abiding by a clear set of principles that guide the operation of the group and the behavior of individual members within the group.

References

Borden, V.M.H., and Banta, T. W. (eds.) *Performance Indicators to Guide Strategic Decision Making.* New Directions for Institutional Research, no. 82. San Francisco: Jossey-Bass, 1994.

Dunn, J. A., Jr. "Setting up a Data-Sharing Project." In P. T. Brinkman (ed.), *Conducting Interinstitutional Comparisons.* New Directions for Institutional Research, no. 53. San Francisco: Jossey-Bass, 1987.

Higher Education Publications, Inc. *The 1996 Higher Education Directory.* Falls Church, Va.: Higher Education Publications, Inc., 1995.

Nicklin, J. L. "Cost-Cutting Consortia: Colleges Try New Forms of Cooperation to Cope with Tighter Budgetary Times." *Chronicle of Higher Education,* Apr. 6, 1994, p. A51.

Patterson, F. *Colleges in Consort: Institutional Cooperation Through Consortia.* San Francisco: Jossey-Bass, 1974.

JAMES F. TRAINER is director of the Higher Education Data Sharing Consortium located on the campus of Franklin and Marshall College in Lancaster, Pennsylvania.

This chapter investigates the benefits and potential problems associated with participating in formal inter-institutional data- sharing organizations.

Benefits and Potential Problems Associated with Effective Data-Sharing Consortia

Mary M. Sapp

Every institution of higher education engages in some form of data sharing, if in no other way than as a result of external requirements to submit data to the U.S. Department of Education's Integrated Postsecondary Education Data System (IPEDS) and other governmental agencies, and in response to surveys from college guidebooks and from various higher education associations. Despite complaints from institutions about the burden associated with responding to these external requests, many institutions have elected to engage in additional data sharing on a voluntary basis in order to have access to data that can be used to improve planning and to inform decision making within the institution. Information about peer institutions can be so valuable that Middaugh, Trusheim, and Bauer (1994) identify inter-institutional peer analyses, together with general data collection and reporting, enrollment management, assessment, and budget support, as the five key responsibilities of an institutional researcher.

Assessments of effectiveness, efficiency, and quality are often couched in terms of how well a school compares with peer institutions. Furthermore, boards of trustees and governmental agencies are increasingly asking for comparative data for evaluation and accountability purposes, and comparative data are often used to justify requests for enhanced funding allocations. In addition, the quality movement in higher education has heightened awareness about the benefits of *benchmarking* (identifying exemplary organizations with the goal of adapting their best practices to one's own institution).

The most systematic efforts involving data exchange are those associated with formal consortia composed of institutions that share data dealing with selected areas of interest and hold meetings on a regular basis. Formal consortia are marked by a stable membership of institutions that often share the same institutional characteristics (for example, mission, control, and size). These consortia generally provide access to an array of data on a variety of topics. They may also produce a standard set of reports. Most have a mechanism and atmosphere that support ad hoc requests (often via e-mail) and the development of reports of special interest. Some formal consortia require dues in order to employ staff who collect data and prepare reports; others share data-collection and report-preparation responsibilities among member institutions. Some are incorporated with bylaws; others have a less formal structure.

Benefits to the Institution

Participating in a data-sharing organization can be advantageous to an institution in a number of ways.

Access to Data for Comparison with Similar Institutions. The most obvious benefit of participation in an ongoing or formal data exchange is that members have access to data from similar institutions to compare with information about the performance of their own institution. Indeed, creating access to data is the raison d'être for such consortia. Of course, for the information to be useful the set of institutions supplying the data must be appropriate.

Usually when an institution selects other institutions with which to compare itself, it refers to them as a peer group, but often they represent either an aspiration group masquerading as a peer group or competitor group, or they are drawn from one of four types of predetermined groups—a preexisting natural group (reflecting, for instance, geographical location or conference membership), an institution's long-standing traditional comparison group, a jurisdictional group (for example, schools from within the same state), or a group of schools with similar institutional classifications (such as Carnegie classification or the American Association of University Professors classification). For more information about the taxonomy, see Brinkman and Teeter (1987) and Teeter and Brinkman (1992).

Some institutions, preferring to rely less on judgment, tradition, and *threshold models* (Terenzini, Hartmark, Lorang, and Shirley, 1980), heave dveloped more objective, data-driven techniques for selecting peers (Brinkman and Teeter, 1987; Rawson, Hoyt, and Teeter, 1983; Teeter and Christal, 1987; and Terenzini, Hartmark, Lorang, and Shirley, 1980). Although such methodologies may be useful for selecting peers in the absence of a consortium, or for selecting a subset of consortium members to include in institutional reports, usually the reality of consortium membership is that the decision about which institutions to include in a report is limited by who is a member and who has submitted data for that particular report. In other words, a formal data-sharing consortium provides another type of preexisting natural group.

Consortia reports often provide normative data that allow an institution to identify areas in which it is doing well and areas where improvements are needed. Comparative data can be used to support (or disprove) intuitive impressions about the institution, particularly with regard to how well it measures up to others. For planning purposes, comparative data are also very helpful. Although longitudinal data for an institution are valuable in and of themselves, trends of aggregate peer data provide an additional perspective for interpreting performance over a given time period. Similarly, although it is useful to know how services and departments are rated by students, it is even more useful to know how these institutional ratings compare with ratings from other schools (for example, is food service rated low because all students tend to give low ratings to this area or is the rating at a particular institution significantly lower than ratings of food service at other institutions?).

For universities and colleges involved in the quality movement, access to peer data allows *performance benchmarking,* or comparing the performance of one's own institution in specific areas with that of others. Several efforts—perhaps most notably the benchmarking project of the National Association of College and University Business Officers—have been undertaken to collect benchmark data relating to a wide range of areas within colleges and universities. Once institutions with superior performance have been identified, their processes can be evaluated (*process benchmarking*) and adapted in order to improve the performance of the institution engaged in the study (Stralser, 1995). Information from data-sharing consortia can be used to identify *improvement gaps* and then, after processes have been modified, to monitor whether the performance has in fact improved. The personal contacts that are made through participation in a consortium can prove invaluable in benchmarking activities as they may help open doors for campus visits at other institutions. This can be especially important in facilitating process benchmarking.

Because many of the data commonly shared by consortia are available from other sources, the question arises, why not just use those other sources? There are four answers to that question: 1) accuracy and comparability of consortium data, 2) timeliness of reports, 3) opportunity to design reports and data collection instruments, and 4) confidentiality of data.

Accuracy and comparability of consortium data. As Steve Stecklow pointed out in a recent Wall Street Journal article (April 5, 1995), the data provided to guidebooks and other media (such as the *U.S. News & World Report*) are often not computed in the same way by all institutions (some schools, for instance, exclude subsets of students with low scores from the computation of their average SAT scores). For data sharing to be valid, reporting must employ comparable data definitions and methodology, include or exclude the same subgroups from the analysis, and measure data from the same period of time in the academic year. Unfortunately, the data that institutions submit to various data collecting organizations occasionally fail to meet these standards and there are few, if any, protections against invalid data. Thus, to help make inter-institutional comparisons valid, data-sharing consortia typically devote a great deal of attention to developing data definitions and decision and counting rules, and to creating data collection forms and accompanying instructions. Also, because institutions within data-sharing consortia tend to be similar, their data are apt to be more comparable, and access to longitudinal data helps to identify reliability problems.

Timeliness of reports. Many consortia include as part of their data collection efforts reporting instruments developed by federal agencies or professional associations (such as standard IPEDS data and the development data collected by the Council for Aid to Education (CFAE)). Often data from these agencies are not available in a timely manner. Consortia, on the other hand, are able to release reports within a couple of months or even weeks, and often data are available electronically as well as in hard copy, thereby speeding up the preparation of individualized reports produced by the institution.

Opportunity to design reports and data-collection instruments. Although existing national data-collection reports provide an important foundation of data about other institutions (see Christal and Wittstruck, 1987, for a comprehensive list of these reports), they generally do not contain the information that institutional researchers need to address a number of important planning and assessment issues (for example, institutional effectiveness, productivity, and optimal allocation of financial aid). The adaptability and flexibility of data-sharing consortia, however, often allow them to supplement existing reports with custom-designed surveys, data bases, and reports that address current issues considered relevant in any given year. Most consortia also encourage members to poll other member institutions informally via e-mail, often about policy- or process-related questions.

A common complaint heard from institutional researchers and others who have to complete outside surveys is that the reporting requirements and instructions for certain surveys are not clear or that the surveys ask for the wrong information (consider, for example, the controversy surrounding the proposed methodology relating to the Student-Right-to-Know Act). In data-sharing consortia, however, member institutions are instrumental in deciding which data to share, in designing data-collection instruments, and in modifying or dropping surveys as they see fit. Having this type of control over work assignments is much more professionally fulfilling than having to respond to a nonnegotiable request from outside.

Confidentiality of data. One final attraction of sharing data through a consortium is that data are treated confidentially. This confidentiality permits data to be shared in a format that identifies each institution—although some highly sensitive data may be distributed in such a way that institutional identity is masked—without raising concerns that shared data will be misused. A bond of trust is developed across institutional participants.

Consortia practice the golden rule of data sharing: Only those institutions that have contributed data can see a data-sharing report or have access to the data base generated as a result of the project. If an institution is unsure how it compares with others on a given measurement, it is reassuring to know that findings will be shared only within this confidential environment. Furthermore, if an institution finds that it inadvertently does not use the same methodology as everyone else, corrections can be made so that erroneous and misleading data will not be made public.

Although access to accurate, timely, and confidential data for comparison with similar institutions is an important benefit of participating in a formal data-sharing organization, it is not the sole benefit of engaging in such an activity. Data-sharing groups also provide individual participants with opportunities to work with others in their field of endeavor.

Network of Peers. Perhaps the benefit mentioned most enthusiastically by members of data-sharing consortia is the opportunity to develop a network of colleagues at peer institutions (Sapp, 1994). Most would agree with Middaugh (1990) that "perhaps the greatest resource available to institutional researchers is other colleagues in the field. . . . The capacity to tap into a collegial network of individuals who have faced and solved similar problems is invaluable" (p. 45). Getting to know one's counterparts at other institutions not only attaches faces to names; these personal interactions make individuals more comfortable about calling or e-mailing colleagues with questions about data or to ask for data for a special project. It is human nature to be more willing to do favors for those we know, and sometimes having others willing to do favors for us can be very important when a special request is needed. Furthermore, these colleagues serve not only as sources of information but also as resources for questions related to methodology, analysis, operations, or the myriad of other issues that may arise on the job.

Personal contact also contributes to an atmosphere of trust and candor and inspires cooperation and sharing rather than competition and secrecy. When they know each other well, contacts are more forthright about methodologies actually used in preparing a report. Loyalty to peers in the profession helps counterbalance pressures from within the institution to make the institution look good. As a result, contacts have much more confidence in the accuracy and comparability of data shared within a consortium than in data provided via an anonymous survey.

The consortium allows researchers to tap into the expertise of their colleagues. Those who are most knowledgeable about a given area tend to provide the leadership in developing survey instruments and analyses relating to that area. As a result, members do not need to reinvent the wheel. This is particularly helpful when a professional conference session deals with an analysis relating to an aspect or function of an institution about which some members may not have in-depth knowledge. Conferences in effect provide on-the-job training.

The development of a network of peers also provides the individual researcher with a forum for learning about other institutions and higher education as a whole. Membership in an ongoing consortium having a stable membership and a regular data-collection schedule that deals with a variety of operations within colleges and universities allows members to develop a context in which to interpret data from others in their comparison group. First, because data are collected over a number of years, longitudinal data can be used to see if findings in any given year are an anomaly or instead are consistent with data from earlier years. Furthermore, because a consortium collects information about a wide range of topics, findings from any given area can be supplemented with data from other areas in order to provide a more complete understanding of the issue at hand. Finally, if any institution in the data base appears to be an outlier, the institutional representative for that school can be contacted for an explanation about why his or her institution is so different from the others.

Although many of the exchanges between researchers described above take place on a one-to-one basis, they may also occur within larger groups.

Conferences, Consulting, and Other Services. Formal consortia hold conferences annually or several times per year. Unlike most professional conferences, which concentrate on panels and presentations of papers, conferences for data-sharing consortia tend to be more participatory, practically oriented, and directly relevant to the work of participants. Discussions often deal with new or existing survey instruments and how results can be effectively presented within the institution.

Conferences sponsored by data-sharing consortia usually include a scheduled time at which members talk informally about what is happening at their institutions, providing invaluable environmental scanning opportunities. These sessions provide a forum for learning about the current hot topics at similar universities and colleges. Interestingly, a hot topic at one institution will often become a research topic at other similar institutions soon thereafter. In addition, as data demands from governmental agencies and guidebooks increase, discussions in data-sharing consortia help members better evaluate the appropriateness of new methodologies for measuring success within their sector of higher education.

Because they tend to be smaller and involve individuals who have known one another for a long time, data-sharing conferences often have the feeling of a get-together of old friends more than a professional conference. Presentations are made in a supportive environment and discussions can be quite candid. The similarity of institutions means that results from one institution may be readily applicable to others (conclusions drawn by similar peer institutions are at least worth investigating at one's own institution). Members often cite these conferences as among the most useful and rewarding they attend.

If a consortium actually produces reports in addition to developing and providing access to a data base, the reports often include analyses that can be circulated within the institution with a minimum of additional data manipulation. If further in-depth analysis is desired, data are available on diskette or from a file transfer protocol (FTP) server so that duplicate data entry is unnecessary. In addition, members usually subscribe to a LISTSERV that allows electronic discussion of issues and distribution of impromptu ad hoc surveys (Dunn, 1989). This ability to broadcast a request to a number of similar institutions is an important fringe benefit to those who need to get an answer to a simple data or policy question quickly.

If the consortium has staff, they can offer consulting advice and customized data bases and reports (for a fee, but one that is much less than if an independent consultant were hired). They also can edit the data for outliers; follow up on suspicious-looking, inconsistent, or missing data; and contact an institution in case there is a question about methodology.

Efficiency. At a time when resources are limited, data-sharing consortia can help improve efficiency because data collection, entry, and editing (and in some cases even analysis) can all be done centrally. Furthermore, members do not have to worry about receiving a series of requests from several peers for identical—or at least similar—data. Any new data collection activities or reports that are developed are those that members agree are important but which they would not have the resources to do on their own. Most members would not have the expertise or the resources to design an array of survey instruments and to analyze peer data, but more importantly, individual institutions would find it much more difficult to obtain data from peers in the absence of a consortium. Finally, by using data from a consortium of similar institutions, a member does not have to use data bases or reports containing data for a large number of institutions of little interest to it or spend time removing these institutions from the data base or report. The very nature of a consortium with a well-defined, limited membership facilitates the development of data bases and reports that are shorter and allow individual researchers to concentrate on institutions of interest to them rather than the entire universe of colleges and universities, thus improving both the efficiency and the validity of comparisons.

Potential Problems for the Institution

Although formal data-sharing consortia provide many benefits, it should come as no surprise that they also bring with them potential problems and costs.

Costs in Terms of Time and Money. Membership in a formal data-sharing consortium typically requires payment of a membership fee, conference costs, and costs for any special surveys and customized reports that may be ordered. Though more difficult to measure, costs such as personnel and computing time are also associated with the preparation of surveys sent from the institution to the consortium and with the preparation of reports for distribution within the institution.

A cost to a member institution (in terms of time) is also associated with being able to count on others in the consortium to respond to its information needs. Because the relationship is a reciprocal one, a member is expected to provide data to others in return for the data received from them. As Sanford puts it, "you have to be a peer in order to have peers" (Moss, Reichard, Sanford, and Sapp, 1995). If an institution does not readily provide data for others, it should not expect to receive data from them. In times of limited financial resources and increasing demands for time, these costs can create potential problems, as institutional researchers must make difficult decisions about how their time is best spent. Obviously, any time the researcher invests in data sharing is time that is unavailable for other activities. On the other hand, as indicated in the discussion of efficiency, the costs might actually be lower if the consortium (rather than the institution) does the collection and analysis. If time invested leads to improved decision making and planning at the institution, then the costs can be justified.

Lack of Data from Key Peer Institutions. One of the biggest sources of frustration for institutions participating in data-sharing activities results from the lack of data from certain key institutions that may be of particular interest to a given school. The absence of data can result from two types of situations: 1) the institution of interest is not a member of the consortium; or 2) the institution is a member but does not participate in a particular report of interest.

Key institution is not a member of the consortium. If an important comparison institution is not a current member of the consortium, the member institution can either try to get the other institution to join or collect the data independently. Very often, however, the nonmember institution will not respond to an outside request or, if it does, the data will not be comparable. This problem is obviously exacerbated if several key institutions are missing from the consortium.

Data-sharing consortia tend to include only institutions with certain characteristics (for example, only private institutions or institutions from a certain region). Because of this, the analysis automatically excludes some institutions that may be otherwise appropriate for the report.

Key institution is a member but does not contribute data for the data base or report of interest. The reality is that not all institutions participate in all of the projects undertaken by the consortia to which they belong (after all, membership and participation are voluntary), so key institutions may be missing from the data base or report that the institutional researcher wants to use. Sometimes an institution will not be in the data base when access is granted or in the official report when it is issued, although it will supply data after the deadline. If the consortium notifies members of updates to its data base, then new data can be added as they become available, but such a policy does not resolve the problem of missing information at the time it is needed. Again, peer pressure to participate sometimes works (the establishment of personal contacts can be useful here), but often it does not. If it can be arranged, encouraging a change in the contact office at an institution with a low response rate also can be effective in increasing that institution's participation.

Problems with Data Collection Instrument or Report. Sometimes, despite the best efforts of the members, the instructions for the data collection form are unclear or not well thought out. As a result, data are not comparable, which in turn may lead to invalid comparisons and misleading or erroneous conclusions. When that happens, members can discuss sources of incompatibility and modify future versions of the instrument. Common sense and an intuitive feel for the data help in identifying inconsistencies and in reducing the likelihood of invalid comparisons being used to inform institutional decision making.

When data-sharing consortia produce reports in addition to providing access to data bases, these reports may prove problematic. For instance, it is often difficult for the reports to strike a proper balance between being in-depth and being a manageable length. In addition, members sometimes have trouble interpreting results and determining how ratios used in the report are computed. Executive summaries and explanations of how ratios are derived help make the reports more useful, as does including graphs. In addition, making the data that were used in the report available on a diskette or on an FTP server allows each individual institution the opportunity to produce exactly what it wishes.

Concerns About Whether Institutions Can Be Compared. Some may argue that there is a fundamental problem with any attempt to compare institutions because important differences in mission and structure may invalidate comparisons even when institutions follow the same directions in supplying data. Thus, finding a set of appropriate peers often can be difficult. Joining a consortium of similar institutions reduces (but does not eliminate) these problems, as does learning about the characteristics of member institutions and developing contacts who are willing to explain idiosyncrasies that may arise. To understand similarities and differences among institutions fully, however, requires more than a series of reports.

Because of the variations in how institutions are organized and in how institutional policies, procedures, and methods of reporting affect the data that they submit for comparisons, peer data should be used only as general guides to inform decision making rather than as a panacea. Any comparisons that are made with data from peer institutions should always be analyzed carefully, and counterintuitive findings and outliers should be investigated more fully or deleted from the comparison. It is also very important to realize that any comparisons made with a single institution are not nearly as valid as are comparisons made with a group of institutions. Comparisons are usually most helpful if members can either compare the data from their own institutions with a median or mean from an appropriate group or can develop an indication of their relative ranking within the overall group (Moss, Reichard, Sanford, and Sapp, 1995). In this way, longitudinal data are also very helpful. If a certain pattern holds up over time (and variations resulting from different structures, policies, or methods of reporting have been ruled out), it is probably valid. See "Setting up a Data-Sharing Project" (Dunn, 1987) for further discussion of the comparability problem.

Potential Reduction of Distinctiveness of Institutions. Whiteley and Stage (1987) argue that peer comparisons may play a role "in the homogenization of American colleges and universities," because administrators at an institution will use data to identify and then reduce the differences between their institution and others. The authors argue, however, that rather than focusing only on how the institution compares with the average of the comparison group and then trying to position the institution closer to this average, planners should also use comparative data to identify the institution's unique characteristics in order to create an appropriate market niche for it.

Concerns About Sensitive Data. Because data exchanged through consortia are often sensitive in nature, concerns about protecting confidentiality and not exposing institutional weaknesses—especially to the public and to the competition (and because of the similarity of their members, consortia may include competitors) are common. Consortia address this concern by requiring all members to enforce agreements protecting the confidentiality of data, and by practicing a golden rule that forbids an institution to see another institution's data unless it has first submitted the same data and has agreed to allow it to be shared with other consortium members. Membership agreements often include statements to the effect that members will use consortium data only for internal planning and management and not for external publication and marketing. Although data are intended to be shared with senior administrators and trustees, providing the information to faculty, and especially students, is discouraged.

Of course, if an institution is particularly sensitive about a given set of data, it can choose not to participate—but then it will not be able to see anyone else's data either. Particularly sensitive projects (average salary by rank and discipline, for example) are sometimes reported only in aggregate rather than on an institution-by-institution basis. Furthermore, statistics that may reveal characteristics of individuals (such as data associated with very small sample sizes in a report on faculty salaries) are usually omitted from the report.

Benefits for the Contact Office

The designated contact office, as the institution's primary conduit for data-sharing activities, may experience the following benefits.

Increased Visibility and Perceived Value. Because data-sharing consortia collect information dealing with all aspects of college and university operations, the contact office will find itself expanding its connections within the institution. For instance, most consortia share data dealing with enrollments, admissions, faculty, development, finance, financial aid, research, and many other areas. Thus, the contact office will need to work with the offices that are responsible for these areas. In turn, administrators will learn quickly that the contact office is able to supply comparative data or to conduct quick informal surveys of peers. In the final analysis, if data sharing and benchmarking are valued at an institution, then serving as the contact for a data-sharing consortium will raise the visibility and perceived value of the contact office.

Better Understanding of Problems and Acquisition of Skills. Through conferences and informal discussions with colleagues, the individuals serving as institutional representatives to consortia feel that their understanding of data is enhanced and, as a result, their understanding of their own institutions improves. Consortia encourage in-depth discussion of current problems. Members share national data, but perhaps more importantly, they also share the perspectives of their own institutions about these problems. Consortia deal with a wide range of data and therefore expand the areas of expertise of the individuals serving as contacts. The conferences and reports also provide a means for members to develop new analysis techniques, to enhance technological skills, and to learn effective ways to present data. Because discussions deal with areas of responsibility of all members, these new skills are directly applicable.

Professional Contacts. As mentioned earlier, because of the size and ongoing nature of consortia, institutional representatives find that some of their strongest professional friendships are formed with contacts at other member institutions. These relationships are enriching on both a professional and personal basis.

Potential Problems for the Contact Office

Although contact offices experience many benefits by participating in consortial relationships, this role is not without its potential problems.

Costs in Terms of Time and Money. Concerns about investing time and money are relevant for the contact office as well as for the institution. Serving as a contact for a data-sharing consortium definitely increases the workload of the office. Not only must reports be sent to the consortium, but reports returned from the consortium must be summarized for dissemination within the institution. Increased visibility often leads to additional requests for information. Time spent on data sharing means less time for other institutional research projects. In addition, the funds required for consortium membership dues and conference fees can put a strain on a department's budget if they are viewed as a departmental rather than an institutional expense.

Lack of Institutional Support. Unfortunately, sometimes contact offices are not supported adequately by the institution and their interest in data sharing is not shared by others on the campus. Furthermore, because many reports require cooperation from the other offices on campus that supply the data, getting the needed institutional data by the deadline is sometimes problematic and frustrating. Certain reports, especially those in which the institution does not compare favorably with its peers, may generate controversy and lead to the involvement of the contact office in campus politics. Institutional researchers view data as important information and generally try not to place value judgments on it regardless of whether the data portend what others may see as good or bad news for the institution. Researchers are inclined to believe that the more information one has, albeit some of it potentially unfavorable, the better off one will tend to be when faced with making a decision. Others may not see it that way, thus casting the individual contact office into a potentially difficult political situation when particular data do not show the institution in the best light.

Conclusion

Because institutional membership in a data exchange is voluntary, any decision to participate in a data-sharing consortium requires a weighing of the benefits and costs associated with such a decision (Bloom and Montgomery, 1980). Membership entails a commitment of time and money, a recognition that key institutions will not always be included in reports, an understanding that all comparisons must be made with caution, and a realization that reports will not always be perfect or always lead to positive impressions about the institution. On the other hand, if a college or university is interested in knowing how it compares with similar institutions, a data-sharing consortium provides efficient and timely access to potentially useful comparative data within a confidential environment; it nurtures a network of professional contacts with colleagues at similar institutions who can share the perspective of their institutions; and it offers conferences, the ability to conduct impromptu surveys, and efficient data sharing among institutions with similar missions and interests. Many institutions have found such consortia important sources of information to support their planning and analysis.

References

Bloom, A. M., and Montgomery, J. R. "Conducting Data Exchange Programs." AIR Professional File, no. 5. Tallahassee: Association for Institutional Research, 1980.

Brinkman, P. T., and Teeter, D. J. "Methods for Selecting Comparison Groups." In P. T. Brinkman (ed.), Conducting Interinstitutional Comparisons. New Directions for Institutional Research, no. 53. San Francisco: Jossey-Bass, 1987.

Christal, M. E., and Wittstruck, J. R. "Sources of Comparative Data." In P. T. Brinkman (ed.), Conducting Interinstitutional Comparisons. New Directions for Institutional Research, no. 53. San Francisco: Jossey-Bass, (1987).

Dunn, J. A., Jr. "Electronic Media and Information Sharing." In P. T. Ewell (ed.), Enhancing Information Use in Decision Making. New Directions for Institutional Research, no. 64. San Francisco: Jossey-Bass, 1989, pp. 73–84.

Dunn, J. A., Jr. "Setting up a Data-Sharing Project." In P. T. Brinkman (ed.), Conducting Interinstitutional Comparisons. New Directions for Institutional Research, no. 53. San Francisco: Jossey-Bass, 1987.

Middaugh, M. F. "The Nature and Scope of Institutional Research." In J. B. Presley (ed.), Organizing Effective Institutional Research Offices. New Directions for Institutional Research, no. 66. San Francisco: Jossey-Boss, 1990.

Middaugh, M. F., Trusheim, D. W., and Bauer, K. W. Strategies for the Practice of Institutional Research: Concepts, Resources, and Applications. Tallahassee, Fla.: Association for Institutional Research and North East Association for Institutional Research, 1994.

Moss, M. K., Reichard, D. J., Sanford, T. R., and Sapp, M. M. "Benefits and Potential Problems Associated with Effective Data Sharing." Panel presentation at the AIR Forum, Boston, May 31, 1995, and at the Southern Association for Institutional Research/Society for College and University Planning Conference, San Antonio, October 11, 1994.

Rawson, T. M., Hoyt, D. P., and Teeter, D. J. "Identifying 'Comparable' Institutions." Research in Higher Education, 1983, 18 (3), 299–310.

Sapp, M. M. "Benefits, Potential Problems and Solutions, and Techniques for Effective Reporting." Breakout session at conference of the Higher Education Data Sharing Consortium, June, 1994.

Stecklow, S. "Colleges Inflate SATs and Graduation Rates in Popular Guidebooks." The Wall Street Journal, Apr. 5, 1995, pp. 1, 8.

Stralser, S. "Benchmarking: The New Tool." Planning for Higher Education, 1995, 23 (3), 15–19.

Teeter, D. J., and Brinkman, P. T. "Peer Institutions." In M. A. Whiteley, J. D. Porter, and R. H. Fenske (eds.), *The Primer for Institutional Research*. Tallahassee, Fla.: The Association for Institutional Research, 1992.

Teeter, D. J., and Christal, M. E. "Establishing Peer Groups: A Comparison of Methodologies." Planning for Higher Education, 1987, 15 (2), 8–17.

Terenzini, P. T., Hartmark, L., Lorang, W. G., Jr., and Shirley, R. C. "A Conceptual and Methodological Approach to the Identification of Peer Institutions." Research in Higher Education, 1980, 12 (4), 347–364.

Whiteley, M. A., and Stage, F. K. "Institutional Uses of Comparative Data." In P. T. Brinkman (ed.), *Conducting Interinstitutional Comparisons*. New Directions for Institutional Research, no. 53. San Francisco: Jossey-Bass, 1987.

MARY M. SAPP is director of Planning and Institutional Research at the University of Miami in Coral Gables, Florida, and chair of the Higher Education Data Sharing Consortium's Board of Directors.

This chapter develops a typology of various data-sharing models. Defining issues in the identification of data-sharing models include organizational purpose and structure, the regularity of the report production schedule, and individual institutional participation criteria.

Data-Sharing Models

Susan M. Shaman, Daniel Shapiro

The computer age, and the extensive storage and rapid retrieval of information it has ushered in, has transformed the way institutions regard data. Today, data are no longer considered solely the inputs and outputs of business transactions; they also are viewed as an institutional resource much the way fiscal, physical, and human capital assets are.

Like all complex organizations, institutions of higher education must be able to assess their current position and evaluate the effects of policy decisions. Data, appropriately summarized and analyzed, provide valuable insights into an institution's progress in meeting its planning aspirations and strategic goals. In particular, time-series comparisons and appropriate ratios provide strategic indicators and benchmarks that help explain an institution to itself. It is this need to provide support for decision making that led to the creation of the institutional research function at campuses across the country.

Institutional leaders today require information about a spectrum of input and output variables, such as student preparedness and enrollment profiles, faculty composition and costs, and learning outcomes. For example, an institution wishing to measure its progress toward building a diverse faculty may ask, How many women are tenured faculty today compared with five years ago and ten years ago? or What is the ratio of minority students to minority faculty compared with the ratio of majority students to majority faculty? Answers to these questions may provide a good understanding of an institution's progress toward its own aspirations.

While institutions may be able to amass and analyze their own information, without good comparative data, institutions lack the normative measures with which to assess the efficacy of policies and practices. The increasing need for peer comparisons to provide a context for their own analyses has prompted institutions to initiate the practice of data sharing. Today, because information is easily stored and easily transferred, data sharing is more practical than ever. Yet, because business practices and information standards vary widely across higher education institutions, data sharing is often difficult. In addition, since some information is proprietary and some information is restricted by statute and legal precedent, data sharing remains complex.

The past several years have witnessed the growth of data sharing among postsecondary institutions. As data sharing has spread and grown in importance, different ways of organizing that activity have emerged.

Dimensions of Data-Sharing Practice

The practice of data sharing varies widely according to the purpose, rhythm, and nature of the participants in the activities. To describe the different data-sharing paradigms, a set of eleven process attributes—dimensions—are proposed. Taken together, the variables describing these dimensions serve to differentiate one data-sharing model from another.

Primacy of Purpose (Primary versus Incidental). Data-sharing entities are differentiated along this dimension according to whether or not the exchange of information is the primary rationale for the process or the primary activity of the organization. Although there are membership organizations or informal associations whose raison d'être is information exchange (for example, the Higher Education Data Sharing Consortium (HEDS) and the College Information Systems Association (CISA), data are frequently shared within organizations whose main purpose is political, social, or other (for instance, various state-wide sector-specific associations of institutions or the Association of American University Professors' (AAUP) annual faculty compensation study). Data collected for objectives other than sharing—regulation and oversight, for example—may be made available subsequently as a secondary effect of the process.

Formality of Arrangements (Formal versus Informal). Some organizations engaging in data sharing are formally chartered and governed. However, considerable data sharing occurs through informal networks and ad hoc structures (see the list of various Association for Institutional Research (AIR) Forum session papers included in Appendix B of this volume for samples of ad hoc data-sharing arrangements).

Control of Process (Internal versus External). Sharing models may be differentiated based on the power exercised by the participants to determine what elements are to be shared, how often data will be collected, and what definitions are to be applied to those elements. Government and other agencies, for example, often foster data sharing by providing the framework for defining, collecting, and disseminating data. Data-sharing associations, on the other hand, may develop elaborate consultative processes for determining how and what to compile and distribute.

Regularity of Activity (Regular versus Occasional). Information can be collected and exchanged according to regular cycles or on an occasional, ad hoc basis. Data-exchange networks and agencies alike use both schemes to acquire and distribute information.

Scope of Information (Multitopical versus Specific Focus). Although some associations and agencies are frequently interested in and share data concerning many facets of the academy, some data exchanges focus on particular areas of interest, such as faculty salaries or fundraising (both the AAUP compensation study and the Council for Aid to Education's (CFAE) voluntary support study are examples of exchanges with a limited focus). Other organizations, such as HEDS, however, share data on an array of topics.

Heterogeneity of Participants (Heterogeneous versus Homogenous Institutions). Some data exchanges, particularly those promulgated by external agencies and governments, involve institutions from all facets of American higher education. Others limit participation to institutions that share a common set of characteristics. Frequently, institutional control, Carnegie classification, geography, religious affiliation, price, and size are among the elements that determine participation.

Membership Criterion (Invitational versus Mandatory). Much data sharing occurs among institutions that have entered into voluntary compacts. Frequently, associations are developed with a few members and extended through invitations to a larger audience (the Consortium on Financing Higher Education (COFHE) and HEDS are examples of organizations whose members are by invitation only). In these associations, membership may change over time as institutions choose to drop in or drop out of the organizations. By contrast, some data submission and ultimate sharing, such as that which occurs under the auspices of regulatory bodies, is mandatory for institutions meeting particular criteria (this type of data sharing would include mandatory submission of Integrated Postsecondary Education Data Survey [IPEDS] forms and the collection of data about institutions by state level agencies).

Number of Partners (Bilateral versus Multilateral). Data sharing is commonly discussed in terms of consortial arrangements and wide-ranging surveys; however, it is also conducted on a bilateral institutional basis. This kind of arrangement, almost always ad hoc, is highly dependent on networks of individuals who can contact their counterparts at other institutions to obtain requisite information.

Openness (Anonymity versus Public Identification). Institutions often are unwilling to exchange sensitive data unless their institutional identities are protected. To accomplish this, some associations report only pooled data. Others encode members' identities so that the casual report reader cannot distinguish among the participants. However, so many data elements are a matter of public record that the need for confidentiality is frequently obviated. Either by agreement of the parties, or through government mandate, a considerable amount of information is exchanged openly.

Media of Exchange (Paper versus Electronic). Data-sharing arrangements may be differentiated according to the extent to which technology is employed to enhance the exchange and dissemination process. Despite the advances in technology, a great deal of information continues to be collected and distributed on paper. Albeit slowly, some data-sharing organizations are promoting and facilitating electronic information exchange. Some enterprises prepare and provide data on diskettes, but the most advanced ones take advantage of the increasingly dependable Internet and Electronic File Transfer Protocol (FTP) to ship and receive data.

Provision of Analysis (Data Analyzed versus Simple Tabulation). Data-sharing entities differ in terms of the sophistication of the analysis included in the reports provided. Reports may contain only simple tables of data or they may contain descriptive and summary statistics, charts, and graphs. The analytic capacity of the institution or organization supplying and reporting the data varies widely. The needs of the membership and purposes of the data collection also play a role in determining whether statistical methods are employed in order to better organize and illuminate the data.

Eleven dimensions might suggest that there could be a large number of different data-sharing models. However, there are a handful of commonly observed practices in information exchange, and they are the ones of greatest interest.

Forms of Data Exchange

Data sharing involving higher education can be divided into two domains—data exchanged with entities and organizations such as state and federal agencies, which exist outside the higher education community, and exchanges within the educational community, which are generally controlled by participating institutions.

With External Organizations. Although one usually thinks of data sharing in terms of a model in which the initiators of, and participants in, the exchanges are institutions of higher education, much of the data that institutions compile and disseminate are shared with those outside academe. As major financial supporters of higher education, federal and state governments are also major requesters and recipients of institutional data. So, too, are other external entities that function as public watchdogs—accrediting agencies, the media, and various educational organizations. Much of the information collected by these external organizations becomes part of the public record. Although these data exchanges are neither convened nor organized by peer institutions, they may serve effectively to facilitate data sharing by defining data elements and then making institution-level data available to all interested parties. These external exchanges can be grouped into three main categories.

Federal agencies. The federal government has been collecting a standard set of data about higher education since the mid-1960s. Begun as the Higher Education General Information Survey (HEGIS) and transformed in 1986 into the Integrated Postsecondary Education Data Survey (IPEDS), these data-collection programs have covered such areas as finance, enrollments, degree completion, teacher preparation, and program offerings. These data are available in a number of formats, including magnetic tape, CD-ROM, and via FTP. In addition to the IPEDS data collected by the United States Department of Education's National Center for Educational Statistics, other federal organizations such as the National Research Council and the National Science Foundation (NSF) collect various data in a number of areas as well. The NSF, through its CASPAR (Computer Aided Science Policy Analysis & Research) data base on CD-ROM, provides a collection of IPEDS, NSF, and other federal report information spanning more than fifteen years.

The press. Higher education generated scarce interest on the part of the media at large until recent years. Most widely available information about higher education was disseminated through parochial organs—the *Chronicle of Higher Education, Academe, Change,* and the like. Today, higher education has become good press. An obvious instance of this is the *U.S. News & World Report* annual rankings of colleges and universities. Issues of methodological consistency and accuracy aside, ranking higher education is a high profile (and high profit) exercise for *U.S. News* as well as for *Money* magazine. Compilation of the data to complete the *U.S.News* and *Money* surveys has become part of the annual institutional research ritual. To this activity can be added the assembly of data for the seemingly unending stream of college guides.

Although data for these publications are prepared specifically for external agents, they nevertheless provide colleges and universities with extensive information about applicant pools, admissions, student quality, costs, faculty, and programs.

State agencies for public institutions. State boards of regents and departments of higher education collect considerable data from and about the public institutions they govern and support. These detailed data are frequently published and may provide comparisons for institutions within a state system.

Within the Educational Community. As the examples in the previous sections show, much institutional data can be shared as a result of the data collection activities of organizations external to the educational community. However, there are several shortcomings to information obtained through these sources. The accuracy of the information provided to external organizations is uncertain for many reasons. Data bound for guidebooks, for example, may (unfortunately) be shaped more for their public relations value than for their analytic value. Moreover, data definitions provided by external requesters are often unclear or ambiguous, and there is no process in place either to resolve such issues or to annotate special circumstances. Thus, to help maximize the utility of shared information, colleges and universities must coordinate and control the data-sharing process.

By crafting information exchanges for specific purposes within the educational community, a relatively high degree of data accuracy can be obtained. By working within a cooperative and collegial forum, issues related to differences in data definitions may either be reconciled or recognized.

Intra-institutional data sharing. A special case of information exchange takes place not between institutions, but within a given college or university.

At universities housing several colleges or schools, there are often obstacles to comparing one school to another based on different business practices, missions, and data definitions. Even at small liberal arts colleges, it is no trivial matter to ensure that useful information is available and accessible to all those who need it. This is due to the increasingly complex nature of the business of education on the one hand, and the increasingly specialized division of labor needed to run the institution on the other. Although intra-institutional data sharing is not the focus of this chapter, it should be pointed out that a major responsibility for most institutional research professionals is to facilitate or implement precisely this type of information exchange.

Inter-institutional data sharing. Inter-institutional data exchange within the educational community is facilitated through three general types of cooperative arrangements. The first of these includes data sharing that is coordinated by already existing organizations whose primary focus is not necessarily the exchange of data, but who collect and share data in specific areas of interest. Examples of organizations in this category include the AAUP, the College and University Personnel Association (CUPA), the CFAE, and the National Association of College and University Business Officers (NACUBO), to name but a few. The second type of inter-institutional data-sharing arrangement is made up of organizations that exist specifically to share data across a broad array of topics or that at least see data sharing as one of their primary functions. COFHE and HEDS are two prime examples of organizations designed specifically to share data. The final type of inter-institutional data-sharing organization is composed of nonconsortial arrangements that are designed to bring institutions together to share data on a specific topic.

Describing models of information exchanges among institutions is the primary focus of this chapter. We will examine in some depth those exchanges that are controlled or coordinated by actors within the community of higher education. Our discussion will focus on the types of organizations in the latter two arrangements described above.

Examples of Data Sharing

Having laid out the dimensions along which data sharing can vary, we now turn our attention to describing an illustrative set of information exchanges that can be found in practice (see Table 3.1). The following descriptions of a selected set of information exchanges enable us to illustrate how data sharing currently works and how it is arrayed along the dimensions described earlier.

Consortial Arrangements. A common model for exchanging information takes the form of an explicit association of institutions. Often the reason for the association has to do with issues other than data sharing, such as curricular, political, or social issues. However, in some cases exchanging information is the primary purpose for the institutions coming together. Although consortia perhaps embody the most formal data-sharing arrangements, they also facilitate a considerable number of informal and ad hoc information exchanges.

Table 3.1. Illustrative Data-Sharing Models Dimensions of Data Sharing

	Data Sharing Purpose of Org or Activity	Nature of the Data-Sharing Structures	Definer of Process/Data vis-à-vis User	Calendar	Scope of Surveys	Partipants	Initiative	Medium for Submission of Data	Medium for Receipt of Reports	Analytic Reports	Institutional Anonymity
A	P: Primary	F: Formal	I: Internal	R: Regular	M: Multi-topical	H: Homogeneous	V: Voluntary	P: Paper	P: Paper	D: Data compilation	O: Open
B	S: Secondary	I: Informal	E: External	P: Periodic	S: Specific	V: Varied	M: Mandatory	E: Electronic	E: Electronic	A: Analysis	C: Coded
C	I: Incidental			O: Occasional		M: Modified heterogeneous	B: By invitation	O: Other media (phone)	O: Other media (phone)	N: No report	G: Group means
IPEDS	I	F	E	R	M	V	M	P	P	N	O
HEDS	P	F/I	I	R/P/O	M	M	B	P/E	P/E	D/A	O/C/G
COFHE	S	F	I	R/P/O	M	H	B	P/E	P	D/A	O/C/G
AAUDE	P	F	I	R/P/O	M	H	B	P	P	D	O
MAC	S	F/I	I	R/P/O	M	H	B	P	P	D	O
CUPA	S/I	F	E	R	S	V	V	P	P	D	O
CFAE	S/I	F	E	R	S	V	V	P	P	D	O
ARL	S	F	I	R	S	H	B	P	P/E	D/A	O/G
Multischool campus	P	F	I	R/P/O	M	H	ALL	ALL	ALL	A/D/N	NR

The mere fact that institutions have an explicit organizational link increases the likelihood that they will contact one another for specific pieces of information.

The consortia described below have some common characteristics. At least part, if not all, of the information exchanges they support take place in a formal and structured manner. Even though a central staff often aids in the administration and development of data collection instruments, the end users of the data—the member institutions—define the processes to be examined and the data to be collected. A regular data-collection schedule is common to their modes of operation, although some consortia supplement this activity with other periodic and occasional data exchanges. The data sharing spans a range of topics. Membership in consortia is usually by invitation or, at least, is determined by well-defined parameters.

HEDS. The Higher Education Data Sharing Consortium (HEDS) grew out of the Tufts-EDUCOM data-sharing project begun in 1983. This group was one of the first consortia whose primary purpose was the efficient exchange of a wide variety of data among a large set of institutions. The HEDS membership includes privately funded colleges and universities. The institutions run the gamut from small liberal arts colleges (Carnegie classification BAI) to major research universities (RI and RII).

The HEDS mission continues to be the support of institutional information exchanges. Among its formal data-sharing activities, the HEDS office collects information on finances, admissions, financial aid, fundraising, and retention. For many data-collection efforts, the consortium merely asks institutions to submit surveys they have completed for other purposes. For example, the IPEDS institutional characteristics and finance surveys are collected by HEDS, as are the NACUBO Endowment and CFAE Voluntary Support surveys. While HEDS institutions are expected to participate in most of the data-collection efforts, participation is voluntary. HEDS restricts dissemination of the school-level data it collects to those member institutions that submit information on a given topic. In the reports compiled by HEDS, schools are explicitly identified, but it is understood that such information will be used cautiously on campus and will not be distributed outside the HEDS consortium. In addition to standard data-exchange activities, HEDS also coordinates and facilitates special activities, such as an annual senior survey. HEDS special analysis reports usually provide comparative data in an aggregated form.

HEDS began using electronic media from its inception. At that time, the technology was cumbersome and most member institutions had neither the staff nor the time to take advantage of the systems. To its credit, HEDS adapted to institutional requirements while continuing to follow technology advances. Today, HEDS is at the forefront in using modern telecommunications technology to support informal and ad hoc information exchanges. HEDS maintains an electronic discussion group where any member institution can post a request to all other members. A HEDS FTP server enables member institutions to electronically access all survey data as well as other useful information, such as a series of national indicators and indexes and data on the baccalaureate origins of Ph.D. recipients.

Data can be provided to HEDS either in paper or electronic form. The HEDS office compiles submitted data, analyzes them, and returns the analyses to members on paper in the form of reports and on diskette or through the FTP server as spreadsheets.

COFHE. The Consortium on Financing Higher Education (COFHE) has a current membership of thirty-one highly selective colleges and universities. It grew out of a 1972 Sloan Foundation study group (Dunn, 1987). The central mission of COFHE is to help its members find creative ways to reduce the cost of higher education and to help students obtain the funds they need to pursue their education. While data sharing is an important benefit of COFHE membership, it is not the primary mission of the organization. Nonetheless, periodic and occasional data-collection efforts on a variety of topics supplement an annual exchange of retrospective information on admissions, tuition and fees, and financial aid. Data are submitted to COFHE in either paper or electronic form. The consortium provides both data compilation and analyses that are distributed to member institutions in the form of written reports. In the past, annual studies identified participating schools explicitly and restricted report use to the senior management of member institutions. As a result of data leakage, these reports, as well as special COFHE studies such as the senior survey, the alumni survey, and the graduation rate study, now contain encoded institutional identities.

In addition to its work in data sharing, COFHE also organizes special forums that bring together institutional representatives to share their experiences and expertise. For example, recent forums have addressed such issues as total quality management, ways to measure faculty teaching and work load accurately, and the administration of student surveys.

GLCA. The Great Lakes Colleges Association (GLCA) was chartered in 1962 as a consortium of twelve midwestern liberal arts colleges. The common characteristics of these institutions are high academic standards and high levels of achievement among both faculty and students. All have a philosophical commitment to the liberal arts and sciences. The mission of the GLCA is to preserve and strengthen its member institutions as private colleges of liberal arts and sciences.

Data sharing is a secondary function of the consortium. The information shared within the consortium is limited to that available through standard public sources. However, GLCA members are able to gain early access to the data for their peers. In general, the heads of functional offices are responsible for exchanging information relevant to their particular areas. For example, the GLCA registrars exchange information on student characteristics, the admissions directors share numbers on a monthly basis, and the business officers are responsible for financial information. In addition, the heads of functional areas meet as a group once a year in annual conferences.

The medium for data exchanges within the GLCA is primarily paper. The GLCA office does not compile or analyze the exchanged data. Rather, the functional leaders at the member institutions manipulate the comparative data on their own.

MAC. The Mid-America Conference membership consists of several institutions in the Midwest, primarily in Ohio and Michigan, but also including Ball State in Indiana. The institutional research offices of the ten member institutions exchange IPEDS information. As is the case for other consortia, MAC institutions form a casual network that can provide comparative data on an as-needed basis.

One rather formal data exchange administered under the auspices of the MAC is a faculty salary study. This study is conducted by the Offices of Institutional Research and Academic Assessment at Ball State University. Members provide Ball State with diskettes containing detailed faculty salary information. The data are then reformatted and entered into a data file. Ball State creates a report that gives overall school comparisons, average salaries by discipline and rank, average salaries for new hires, and descriptive data of faculty by discipline. Ball State has contributed the work of analyzing the data and compiling the report, and also performs special studies for other MAC schools if requested. In return, the Ball State IR office has access to a data base containing 7000 cases of microlevel data on faculty salaries and characteristics spanning a ten-year period.

AAUDE. The Association of American Universities Data Exchange (AAUDE) has as its primary purpose the annual exchange of faculty salary and teaching load data. In addition, other information of mutual interest to the institutional representatives is exchanged. The AAUDE was organized in 1973 by interested presidents of the Association of American Universities (AAU). The AAUDE operates informally and has no formal connection to the AAU, but it does use AAU membership as a criterion for participation in the exchange (*AAUDE Practices,* 1992).

The AAUDE is essentially an exchange of paper documents, many of which would have been compiled for other purposes. These include the AAUP faculty salary survey, as well as IPEDS enrollment, financial, degree completion, and staff reports. A wide breadth of additional information—factbooks, organizational charts, tuition and fees data, admissions statistics, data on administrative salaries, departmental expenditures, and more—is also exchanged. Except for information like the IPEDS data, which is of the public record, shared information is confidential outside of the AAUDE, with institutions identified only by codes.

Although no central agency provides an analysis or compilation of the exchanged data, summaries and reports that contain AAUDE "all institutions" and "all disciplines" data are provided to AAUDE representatives by other volunteer AAUDE institution representatives (for example, the University of Virginia provides consortium summaries of salary data from the College and University Personnel Administration salary surveys and the University of Maryland provides summaries of IPEDS faculty salaries information) (AAUDE, 1993).

IVY-IR. Beginning in 1987, representatives from the eight Ivy League schools, MIT, and Stanford have met annually at the campus of one of the member institutions to discuss institutional research issues. In addition to using the informal gathering to discuss current issues related to institutional research on the ten campuses, the representatives share basic information on faculty size, enrollments, and degrees awarded. Throughout the year, the group maintains contact via an electronic discussion group administered by the Princeton registrar. This forum is often used for making ad hoc data requests as well as for sharing relevant news.

Nonconsortial Arrangements. Data sharing is not limited to the kinds of consortial arrangements described above. Other models usually exist for the purpose of sharing information about a specific topic. In some cases an academic institution coordinates the activity, and in others some other interested entity takes on that responsibility.

ARL. The Association of Research Libraries (ARL) is a formal membership organization of more than 100 North American research libraries. Although the membership is dominated by public and private universities, it also includes a handful of other major libraries such as the Library of Congress, the National Library of Canada, and the New York Public Library, that are not affiliated with universities. The organization's purpose is to improve access to and effectiveness of library materials, to promote collaboration among its members, to foster innovation, and to influence information policy.

For a number of years the ARL has been collecting data on library resources, staffing, expenditures, and usage. Annual statistical reports, rich in data and indicating how libraries rank on a variety of measures, are widely shared among the members.

University of Virginia Tuition Survey. Beginning in 1981, the Office of Resource and Policy Studies at the University of Virginia began collecting information on tuition and room and board charges for a selected set of research universities. Since that time, Virginia has taken the lead in compiling and disseminating this information to participating schools. The data are not proprietary and institutions are identified by name. Participants now have more than a dozen years' worth of tuition and fees data available in a single place for peer institutions. The data collection and dissemination are both done in paper form. No analysis of the submitted information is performed; however, by compiling and organizing this information over time a quite useful longitudinal data set has evolved.

National Study of Instructional Costs and Productivity. This project is conducted by the Office of Institutional Research and Planning at the University of Delaware, and underwritten by a grant from the Fund for the Improvement of Post Secondary Education. It involves the collection of detailed information about faculty instructional workloads at the academic discipline level, the instructional expenditures associated with that discipline, and the externally sponsored research and service activity of the faculty. The result is a series of productivity and cost ratios that address issues such as, who is teaching what to whom, and at what cost? In the last completed year, 160 institutions participated including research universities, doctorate-granting universities, comprehensive colleges and universities, and baccalaureate colleges. The Office of Institutional Research and Planning at the University of Delaware analyzes the submissions and compiles a report that allows participants to compare themselves to other institutions.

On the Horizon

The digital technologies that ushered in the era of widespread data storage and data manipulation and that gave rise to the development of institutional research and data sharing are now part of a revolution known as the Internet. The expansion of the net—with the World Wide Web, and browsers that can help locate information at the touch of a button—is changing the paradigm of institutional data sharing. Hundreds of colleges and universities across the country (and the world) have developed home pages that serve as gateways to treasure troves of institutional information. It is possible to gather data from a wide variety of institutions, frequently without their permission or even their knowledge. Institutional researchers can form temporary, ad hoc peer sets to suit their analytic needs.

However, the benefit of open access to a wealth of comparative data is frequently offset by the nature of the data, which may be overwhelming, cumbersome, undocumented, and out of date. Moreover, information that is valuable for its strategic importance is usually protected from public view and is posted with password protection, encryption, or is omitted from the Internet altogether. Ultimately, the Internet may serve as a safe and swift vehicle for posting, annotating, and sharing data among institutions who agree in advance about the nature and limitations of the information. As such, the Internet may serve to facilitate and enhance the efforts of the consortia and organizations described earlier. We are likely to witness an increase in the number of institutions that trade data with their peers, an increase in the level of data-sharing activity, a proliferation of data-sharing arrangements, and evolving paradigms for promoting effective and efficient information exchange.

References

Association of American Universities Data Exchange. *AAUDE Practices.* April 15, 1992; revised April 1994.
Association of American Universities Data Exchange. *Benefits and Purpose of the AAU Institutions Data Exchange (AAUDE).* April 3, 1993; revised April 1994.
Brinkman, P. T. (ed.). *Conducting Interinstitutional Comparisons.* New Directions for Institutional Research, no. 53. San Francisco: Jossey-Bass, 1987.
Dunn, J. A., Jr. "Setting up a Data-Sharing Project." In P. T. Brinkman (ed.), *Conducting Interinstitutional Comparisons.* New Directions for Institutional Research, no. 53. San Francisco: Jossey-Bass, 1987.

SUSAN M. SHAMAN *is assistant vice president for planning and analysis at the University of Pennsylvania, and serves as chair of the Higher Education Data Sharing Consortium's Research Advisory Committee.*

DANIEL SHAPIRO *is director of institutional research at the University of Pennsylvania.*

This chapter examines the cost of establishing a data-sharing exchange and argues that the cost involved in doing so is minimal when compared to the potential cost involved in making decisions without access to good comparative information.

Creating a Cost-Effective Data Exchange

E. Raymond Hackett

The Context for Affordable Information-Sharing Consortia

Institutions of higher education are, by any standard, complex entities. Even the least complex of institutions, the small, residential liberal arts college, provides an enormous number of pedagogical, social, behavioral, and economic phenomena to study. As campus decision makers begin to understand these phenomena, they become more effective at defining and creating the information needed to support decision making. The campus year might be envisioned as multiple threads woven together between outstretched hands, like a cat's cradle. Among these threads are a recruitment and retention thread, an academic programs thread, a student life thread, a staffing thread, a physical plant thread, and a fiscal thread. Like cotton thread, this imaginary thread is made of a number of twisted fibers.

In the real campus year, along each of the threads and fibers lie decision points, the sum of which are instrumental in creating an institution's future. In turn, this chapter examines the costs, financial and otherwise, that institutions invest in reaching good decisions. It also highlights the role that participating in an inter-institutional data-sharing effort can play in helping decision makers arrive at informed decisions.

It is rather easy to list critical decision points in the campus year and the questions they raise:

- What decision rule will we use for admitting students?
- How will financial aid be apportioned?
- Will there be unfunded financial aid, and if so how much?

- Will faculty and staff receive a raise?
- Can maintenance be deferred?
- What programs will be targeted for excellence and at what expense?
- Should resources be diverted to a first-year student experience program?
- Should the training of resident assistants be enhanced?

The answers to these questions, and a myriad of others confronting the campus administrative and planning team, will be cast in terms of decisions.

At the very least, the leadership of every campus must ask the following two questions at the beginning of each academic and planning year. First, will we be intentional in making decisions for this campus? Second, will we use the best possible information to reduce uncertainty before we make decisions? Assuming that decisions are to be intentional, our primary concern then is the need to reduce uncertainty before a decision is made. It is the place of institutional research to provide information that reduces uncertainty prior to making decisions. One way to facilitate this important function is by participating in an active data-sharing group.

Given the costs that may be related to making a bad decision, it would seem that no expense would be spared in support of the decision-making function; thus, the investment that many institutions make in institutional research and in planning and analysis. Unfortunately, these investments are far from universal in higher education. Generally, the more financially stressed an institution feels, the more likely that it will apply minimal support to the institutional research function. Institutions that cannot afford to make poor decisions spend the least to reduce their uncertainty before making decisions! Likewise, institutions that have a feeling of programmatic and financial well-being may not be aggressive in the application of resources to institutional research. Whether rich or poor, institutions that aggressively pursue the reduction of uncertainty share one characteristic. They are afraid of the cost of a poor decision. Fortunately, these unsettling times for the higher education enterprise have instilled fear in many presidents and boards of trustees.

What is the Cost of a Poor Decision? From the outside looking in, the decision to shortchange the uncertainty-reducing function of the decision-making process seems unimaginable. Even small liberal arts colleges have total expenditure budgets of between ten and forty million dollars. Certainly, support for an office of institutional research and dues to a data-sharing association could be found. However, budgets are not built logically; they are built incrementally, and to add resources to one function is to take them away from another. Whatever the total institutional expense budget, it is the sum of all the cost-center budgets. At the cost-center level, budgets are, for all practical purposes, composed of fixed costs. These fixed costs encompass salaries and benefits, supplies, services, and utilities. Adding $2,000 to pay dues to a data-sharing consortia is a major programmatic choice. Adding an office of institutional research is a monumental decision.

Thus, the question might be asked, what is the cost of a poor decision? For instance, what is the cost of setting tuition too high? Or, what is the cost of not understanding the factors that affect retention? These questions might be answered in terms of revenue that goes unrealized. The answer to any of these questions can be significant for the finances of a college or university.

If it is difficult to define problems that can be addressed with quantifiable information, how are less tangible decisions measured? How are pedagogical or student life decisions quantified? In these situations, the field of cost accounting and the obscure notion of *opportunity cost* may be helpful. Opportunity cost is, in essence, the inverse of expenditure. It represents the cost associated with an opportunity lost by expending resources in one way and not another. In terms of decision making, we might ask what opportunity was lost by deciding in favor of one direction over another. For instance, what may be the opportunity cost associated with limiting financial aid expenditures to spend monies elsewhere at the risk of missing enrollment projection targets? Unfortunately, we can never fully measure opportunity costs. We can, however, study institutions that have chosen other paths. Regardless of how we do it, our goal is to make the best decisions possible.

Reducing Uncertainty in Making Good Decisions. One of the ironies in making decisions is that choices are focused on creating the future but the past is all that we have to provide uncertainty-reducing information. Much of the information that can be useful in higher education decision making can be loosely classified as historical, or longitudinal, information on the operations of the institution; information about the operations of similar institutions; and information about potential impacts on the institution from events or trends external to the institution.

The institutional research program at most institutions focuses on information generated about the institution's recent past. Much of the effort focuses on attempts to understand the change over time of key performance indicators. Institutions of higher education, however, cannot be viewed in simple terms. They are large, complex systems comprising a number of subsystems. Any particular data point or piece of information cannot be viewed in isolation. Rather, each element must be thought of in terms of what it represents within a system or subsystem.

The study of higher education is a relatively young discipline, and few attempts have been made to understand the operational behavior of institutions in ways that can be modeled. With few conceptual models for decision making, the value of comparative data increases. The question then becomes, at an equivalent decision point, what happened when a similar college made a certain decision? What was the change in the key performance indicator? Other campuses provide live models of the enterprise. If a campus, for instance, is about to increase the level of unfunded financial aid, the results encountered at a similar institution several years prior would be instructive. In essence, data-sharing associations serve as a surrogate for an adequate causal literature in higher education. Hopefully, the recent growth in data-sharing associations will strengthen the modeling literature in higher education.

Prerequisites to Accurate and Timely Data. Using longitudinal and comparative information requires that accurate and timely data be assembled. There is no easy way around this. Data element definitions must be strictly adhered to over time within the institution and by institutions involved in any data exchange. A data element dictionary must be agreed upon and all of the end data providers on each campus must be carefully trained. Data reporting deadlines should be observed and there should be some formal mechanism for exchanging data between institutions.

In comparing information between institutions, the characteristics of the peer group an institution selects should be carefully considered. Comparisons with like institutions in terms of size, resource availability, academic program, including the mix of traditional and nontraditional programs, and student characteristics must all be taken into account in making valid comparisons. However, comparisons with institutions that are not completely similar are also useful from a modeling perspective. The key performance indicators of a group of institutions perceived as financially or academically stronger might serve as benchmarks to be reached. Decisions might be made that would drive a key performance indicator toward the higher benchmark. Being more selective about the academic credentials of incoming students is one such decision an institution can make. Of course, without a larger pool of students to chose from, such a decision can have adverse financial consequences!

Prerequisites to the Development of an Affordable Data-Sharing Association. The first consideration in creating a data-sharing association is the cost of making poor decisions. As in the concept of opportunity cost, a number of decisions can be made within the annual planning and budgeting cycle where the opportunity cost is unacceptable either in a financial or a mission sense. Any fraction of the financial loss for a poor decision is an acceptable expense for an effective institutional research program. Although it cannot be argued that an effective institutional research function can eliminate poor judgment, it is helpful to understand how data can be used to inform what it is hoped will prove to be good decisions over the long run.

Unfortunately, the culture on most college and university campuses is not focused on opportunity, opportunity cost, or vision. Most campus cultures, like their budgets, have an incremental vision. It is within these cultures that the proponents of a data exchange must highlight the cost of poor decision making and compare that cost to the cost of effective institutional research. Of course, in calling attention to a situation in which better information might have led to a more insightful decision, keep in mind the Turkish proverb, "He who tells the truth should keep one foot in the stirrup."

The last decade has seen the increased acceptance of the concept of *outsourcing* in higher education. Simply put, the campus contracts out a service that could be provided by campus staff in an attempt to increase quality and decrease personnel costs. Insurance, food service management, custodial services, vending, and even payroll processing are services that can be provided to a number of campuses by private companies. The strategy for creating a data-sharing consortium, outlined below, can be likened to outsourcing part of the institutional research function.

Creating a Viable Consortial Arrangement

One way to define a viable data-sharing exchange is by the size and commitment of its membership. Is the association large enough to provide adequate peer comparison groups for the various member institutions and to accommodate some annual turnover in membership? It can be said that for every institution that is part of a data exchange, there is a champion for that association on the campus. The experiences of successful data-sharing associations suggest several characteristics that can serve as a guide for similar efforts.

Sweat Equity. Perhaps the most essential ingredient is a commitment on the part of the founding institutions to the time, effort, and tasks required to bring about a successful association. For instance, in creating a business, the time and effort of the founding principles is called *sweat equity*. Those institutions that have been involved in the creation of a data-sharing association would agree that it is an apt term to describe the work involved by the founding institutions. These institutions must accomplish several key tasks that require a significant amount of time and energy.

1. *Define the opportunity for the data exchange.* There must be a reason for a group of institutions to develop a consortial arrangement. In the context outlined above, that reason would encompass the development of information to help inform the decision-making process and to reduce uncertainty prior to making decisions. Invariably this begins with a campus officer recognizing a number of key decision points that would benefit from historical and peer information. Over time, at professional meetings, these insights are shared with colleagues who have had similar insights and a commitment begins to build to find an ongoing mechanism for a data exchange. Because any action to develop an association of institutions will require time and resources, the various champions of the data exchange must develop enough of a consensus on their own campuses to allow the effort to begin. This initial phase requires insight, discussion, and consensus building.

2. *Identify the peer group.* In the context outlined above, where information from other institutions serves as a model, or benchmark, for decisions to be made on a campus, defining the institutions to be included in the data exchange is an essential exercise. In his book *Higher Education Revenues and Expenditures* (1991), Kent Halstead gives a thorough analysis of this process from the cost perspective. Halstead emphasizes that it is essential to gather information on potential peer institutions prior to beginning the data-exchange process. The Integrated Postsecondary Education Data System (IPEDS) data set maintained by the National Center for Educational Statistics (NCES), even with all the limitations of integrity and timeliness inherent in it, provides a starting point for gathering information about other institutions. Likewise, the National Science Foundation (NSF) has funded a program in the last several years to place a large amount of the NSF and

IPEDS data from 1971 until the present on one CD-ROM. This CD-ROM comes packaged with user-friendly retrieval MS-DOS-based software and is called the Computer Aided Science Policy Analysis & Research Database System (CASPAR). The cost for this CD was $350 at first issue and will probably remain near this level. To obtain the CASPAR CD contact Quantum Research Corporation, 7315 Wisconsin Ave., 631 W, Bethesda, MD 20814. NCES IPEDS data are also now being made available over the Internet directly from the Department of Education. You can reach the Department at URL http://www.ed.gov/. NCES data files can be downloaded from URL gopher://gopher.ed.gov:10000//11/data/postsec/ipeds. (Additional information on the availability of electronic files is included in Appendix A of this volume.)

Key considerations in defining the appropriate institutional members for a data exchange are:

Scale economies. Almost all decisions in higher education have some cost consideration explicitly attached to them. Implicitly, issues related to scale of operation are attached to all decisions. Choosing a peer group that is of some similar scale of operation is usually an important consideration. The economies related to an institution of fifteen hundred students and one with ten thousand are different.

Type and control of institution. Similarities in the programmatic offerings of institutions are usually essential to comparison considerations. In addition, whether institutions are publicly or privately controlled usually provides for significant differences even when controlling for size. The Carnegie Classification system attempts to encompass these differences and to provide definitions for class of institution based on programmatic mix, degree offerings, and size. Though quite useful, both of the recent Carnegie attempts at classification fall short when used to develop a peer group for decision-focused comparisons. Taking into account equivalent type and control of institutions in the Carnegie classification system, level of revenues must be considered. For instance, a Baccalaureate I institution with a $200 million endowment will look quite different from an institution with an endowment of less than $20 million when compared on any number of indicators.

Historical and geographical considerations. Key decision makers, especially board of trustee members, view the institution in its historical or traditional context. This context is part of the decision-making culture on the campus. Therefore, it may be necessary for the institutional research program to deliver comparative information from the historical perspective. Traditional institutional ties could include denomination (if the institution has or had a religious affiliation), state, city, region, or athletic conference, to name a few such considerations. Taken in the context of the other characteristics used to develop peer groups, institutions included for historical purposes may not make sense. But from the perspective of the decision-making culture on campus, information from historically related institutions must be provided.

Dissimilarities. For comparative purposes, institutions that are dissimilar in some ways might provide important information. An institution with a different program mix or scale of operation can provide valuable comparative information, particularly in the sense of a live model. For example, an institution with a traditional student population might be considering programs to serve nontraditional students. What better place to observe the effects of a different programmatic mix than at an institution similar in most ways but this one?

3. *Define the data to be exchanged.* Defining the data that are to be exchanged is an act that follows defining the problems that are to be explored. Most campuses are awash in data that fall out of the daily operation of the institution. Data to explore almost any issue important to the campus can be captured from that daily data stream if there is a clear understanding of the analysis to be conducted. Defining and identifying the data to be exchanged can be seen as a four-part process.

Define the problems to be investigated. The strengths of the inductive-deductive method cannot ignored. Problems must be envisioned, hypotheses developed, and research methodology defined. Unfortunately, much of the information that we use in higher education to reduce uncertainty is used in a visual inspection rather than a truly analytical mode. Reliance on visual inspection (or eyeballing) is unacceptable. We must be more intentional in the study of higher education, in the use of information in the campus context, and in developing a research design mentality. The questions we ask must focus at the system or subsystem level and must include the ability to measure in some way the amount of actual uncertainty that was reduced. In other words, was this information useful in helping us make good decisions?

Identify data that are already being collected. As was mentioned above, a huge data stream flows from the day-to-day operations of institutions. The campus is populated with primary data producers. Many of the research problems faced in higher education can be addressed from data that are available somewhere in that stream. It is incumbent on the institutional research community to be familiar with all of the data being generated on campus at the most primary level.

Identify what must be uniquely defined and collected. The campus data flow may not provide all of the data necessary for an important research problem. In this case there is no other alternative than to collect new data. The institutional researcher should remain acutely aware that it will likely be some primary data provider, with other responsibilities, who will bear the brunt of this data-collection effort. The unique data-collection effort, therefore, must be designed to minimize the impact on the rest of the campus community.

Create a data element dictionary. A data-element dictionary provides an elemental and essential underpinning to any data-exchange effort. A thorough detailing of what is included in a count, what is excluded, and when the count takes place is the single most important guarantee that inter-institutional data will be comparable. In many cases, the count desired will be taking place for some other data collection effort. If an IPEDS form requires the same data, recapitulate the IPEDS definition, elaborate if deemed necessary, and include a reference as to where to find a particular data element. For example: IPEDS F-1 Part A, line 01 (03)

4. *Create a viable exchange strategy.* The strategy used to exchange the data must not be cumbersome to the institutions involved. Ideally, participating institutions should need to send only one paper form, data disk, or electronic transmission of data out to the exchange in order to receive comparative data back from the exchange in a similar format. Some exchanges include a summary report back to the member institutions. Others only provide access to raw data. In either case, for an exchange to be successful, communicating with the exchange should not in practice or perception consume too much time or other resources at the campus level.

Institutions need to realize, however, how much of an investment they are already making in collecting, storing, and providing data even if they do not belong to an active exchange. In turn, data-sharing activities should be designed to take advantage of and maximize the effect of these existing efforts. The campus-level data-collection effort, whether for multiple agencies or for the exchange alone, is a significant effort consuming significant resources. The design of an exchange should be such that it is perceived as supporting and strengthening the campus data collection effort and not adding to it. The exchange can assist institutions by offering training to primary data providers. These staff members have other responsibilities and usually are not trained to think like the institutional research staff. They have some understanding that the data that spin out of their daily work are important to the institution. However, producing data to inform the institution's decision-making process is not their primary concern. Thus, sharing with the appropriate staff information about how these data are used, and training them in the various nuances of the data collection activity may benefit the collection effort itself and possibly campus morale as a whole.

5. *Develop a useful initial product.* Institutions, like people, enjoy seeing a return for their labors. One of the key activities that the founding institutions of an exchange can engage in is developing and producing a data set or report early in the life of the association that is of use to the campus community. No other act will do more to ensure the health and growth of the data exchange. The campus champion of the exchange should be able to demonstrate that the effort can in fact support the campus decision-making process. The long-range, overall payoff to the association may be far greater than that initial product, but without it the association may not survive long enough for the greater reward. This last part of the sweat equity investment may require significant effort.

Finding a Cost-Effective Home

As the data exchange begins to take shape, finding a permanent institutional location for the staff of the association becomes a necessity. Consortial arrangements in higher education can be as simple as having an office at a member institution that provides a mailing address, with the letterhead being the only indication that the association resides at that institution. In this simplest case, the work of the association is coordinated by the association's officers supported by the host institution's office staff. At the other extreme, the association can have its own staff and can be housed in its own unique association office. Obviously, the smaller the permanent staff and overhead costs, the smaller the individual institution's share of the overall expense. The size of the office staff and nonpersonnel budget depends on the scope of the program and work that the member institutions define for the association. It also depends on the amount of the association's work that will be accomplished by the association staff and the amount that will be done at the institutions.

However complex the association office, the most cost-effective strategy is to house it at a member institution. The selected institution should be able to provide office space and utilities without cost to the association or in lieu of dues. In addition, it is helpful if the exchange is able to function under the host institution's administrative umbrella. If the association can be incorporated as an unrestricted current fund or agency-funded project within the host institution's budget, then it can reap the benefits of established business practices, a personnel program, telecommunications, hardware and software discounts, and essentially all the related economies that come with a large scale of operation. Being associated with a member institution also makes it possible for the exchange to use work-study students as part of its labor force.

Another cost-effective strategy for developing an association office with a support staff is to align the association with a university doctoral program. The first step in this process is to identify a faculty member with research interests similar to those of the association. A higher education doctoral program can provide an excellent support structure for a data exchange. All the benefits outlined for housing the exchange at a member institution hold when the exchange becomes an ongoing research project at a university. An added benefit in this approach is the population of doctoral students who can serve as graduate research assistants supporting the research agenda of the exchange, the exchange supporting the students' research interests in return.

Institutions Taking the Lead for Individual Studies. Staff are the largest cost center for a data-sharing association. The scope of the association's activities may include the exchange of raw data, the production of one or more annual reports, and the development of discrete one-time investigations. Certainly, one strategy for accomplishing any program of work would be to hire the staff necessary to accomplish it. Another viable strategy followed by several successful data-exchange associations is to have each member institution take responsibility for one of the specific studies proposed by the membership. In this case, a member institution does the coordination, data collection, and report preparation for all of the institutions involved in an individual study. With this model, it is usual for only those institutions that participate in the study to receive a report. This provides an incentive for institutions to participate without requiring members of the association to participate in research that is not of interest to their institutions.

The Advantages of Modern Machines. The volume of data exchange and information processing in progress around the country is in itself rather difficult to fathom. As short a time as a decade ago the scale of data exchange being pursued today would have required a major institutional commitment of computing resources. However, the processing power of microcomputer hardware and the power and ease of use of software have made these consortial data-exchange efforts possible and affordable.

Although specific hardware and software alternatives are likely to be outmoded before this publication goes to press, several strategies will be mentioned. First, microcomputers in fiscal 1995–96, priced at under $4,000, are capable of processing information for a large-scale organization. Coupled with an appropriate data base and storage medium, they provide input, storage, and analysis capabilities available only on $100,000+ minicomputers or mainframes less than a decade ago. Most platforms now offer true relational data base management software (DBMS) that includes query language, report writing, and graphic capabilities. Several of the major DBMS packages work transparently across platforms and operating systems.

Second, analytical packages have evolved into a combination of spreadsheet, programming language, statistics, and graphics. These software packages (such as Lotus Office Suite or Microsoft Excel) are generally easy to learn and powerful to use. Their graphics are integral to analytic functions and nearly as complete as the most sophisticated graphics packages of a few years ago.

Third, several outstanding statistical packages are available that can be linked with either DBMS or analytical software to allow a full range of classical statistics. Once relegated to large campus mainframes, sophisticated statistical software packages are now not only available on microcomputers but can also be linked to many of the programs already in use.

Once analysis is complete, the presentation of results and comparisons must be done in such a way as to make them useful to the decision-making process. The current generation of word-processing software has outstanding report preparation capabilities and accommodates importing charts and graphs from analytical packages. Desktop publishing software brings the capabilities of a typesetter to the same machine that stores the data and runs the analysis. These packages will accept text from word processing as well as charts and graphs from analytical packages and will produce camera-ready copy.

To reiterate, the low cost and high power of modern computer processing have significantly reduced the personnel and processing costs associated with a multicampus data-exchange effort. Computing is the one area where expense should not be spared. Researchers should invest in a high-end personal computer, mass storage that is expandable, communications software, and a laser printer. The machine should be able to store, retrieve, and analyze data, prepare charts, graphs, and camera-ready copy, and serve as a FAX machine and modem.

The Electronic Consortium—The Net Is the Future. Regardless of where an institution is located, it is most likely that it is already on the net or that Internet access can be made available. Internet and networking availability provides many benefits to a data-sharing organization. For instance, it does not take a large conceptual leap to move from organizational meetings at a site geographically central to institutions to organizing electronically. In addition, setting up a dedicated file server at an association's office and using the net is already a reality with some data exchanges (see Jim Fergerson's chapter in this volume). It will be part of the structure of all such associations in the near future. This statement is not a forecast, it is common sense. However, one should not lose sight of the fact the networks and file servers are not an association of colleges and universities, they are hardware and software. All the work and focus on timely and accurate data are still at the heart of any data exchange. What happens on campus in collecting data, the analysis and use of that data, and making good decisions will remain central to a data- and information-sharing association of institutions. In the near future and thereafter, associations of colleges and universities, especially those focused on data sharing and analysis, will exist predominantly as electronic meeting places.

Conclusion

There is only the future. The decisions made within the yearly planning, budgeting, and activity cycles of the campus define an institution's future. Using the best possible historical and comparative information to reduce uncertainty before making decisions is the responsibility of the decision-making team on every campus. The data-exchange phenomenon is evidence that many campuses understand this reality. In almost every case, the cost of poor decisions far outweighs the cost of accurate and timely information. If institutions are willing to commit to a data-exchange association, even the effort in the initial year is minimal compared to the benefits. Contemporary hardware and software have minimized the cost of accomplishing what still is a sophisticated project. Accurate and timely information supporting the decision-making process is the essential ingredient in defining a desirable future for institutions. In one sense, it might be said that there are two futures, the one we are drifting into and the one we want. It is our task to envision the former and create the latter.

Reference

Halstead, K. *Higher Education Revenues and Expenditures.* Washington, D.C.: Research Associates of Washington, 1991.

E. RAYMOND HACKETT is an assistant professor and executive director of the College Information Systems Association at Auburn University in Auburn, Alabama.

Effective data sharing depends on the proper management and use of technology. This chapter provides a retrospective on the role technology played in the development of a data-sharing organization and describes the types of technologies that are currently emerging and the potential impact these may have on data sharing both within and across institutions.

Data Sharing and Keeping Pace with Changing Technologies

James C. Fergerson

Cooperative data sharing among members of institutional consortia can provide institutional researchers and other administrators with valuable information for use in planning, but at times the additional effort and labor required may seem to outweigh the benefits of the new knowledge and insights obtained from data sharing. Submitting institutional data to others in a common and meaningful format may not be a trivial task. The people charged with organizing and disseminating a shared data set face numerous methodological, definitional, and clerical difficulties. Those receiving the data may face similar problems when trying to translate or read the files. When shared information from a set of institutions is obtained, it is not always in a format that is useful to the key administrators who are the end users of the data. Often considerable editing, analysis, and publishing chores are needed before shared information can be distributed. Each step in the data-sharing process has a cost, and every additional step required in processing information takes time and steepens the learning curve. Every delay reduces the meaning of time-sensitive information.

This chapter discusses some of the techniques that institutions have used and may use in the future to disseminate and share information among themselves, and how technology can both help and hinder the exchange of information.

A Case Study: The HEDS Experiments

One of the first models for consortial data sharing began in the late 1970s and early 1980s with the establishment of the Tufts-Educom Data Sharing project, which was supported on a grant from Exxon (now the member-supported

Higher Education Data Sharing Consortium (HEDS) located on the campus of Franklin and Marshall College). With support from Educom and institutional members, an area on a Cornell University mainframe was reserved where members could share institutional data and use what was at the time very sophisticated budgeting and forecasting software. Before desktop computers came into general use as office tools, and before the advent of electronic spreadsheets, the mainframe-based EFPM (Enrollment Forecasting and Planning Model) software was a godsend to administrators who wished to experiment with complex interactions among budget components and examine the long-range implications of changes in budgets and student enrollments. Members could connect to the Cornell mainframe, invoke EFPM, type in various budget assumptions, and run numerous reports under those various assumptions. Institutions could also share data from the U.S. Department of Education's annual Integrated Postsecondary Education Data System (IPEDS) reports by connecting to Cornell and manually typing in figures from their reports.

From a purely technical standpoint, all of the pieces of the system worked well. From a practical standpoint, however, the model was probably well ahead of its time. The project placed numerous technical obstacles in the path of data providers who were either uncomfortable with computing or who did not have ready access to the required hardware and software. Every step in the process had either a steep learning curve, an inconvenience, or a weak link in the technological chain. At the time, network and modem-based telecommunications were not widely used by college administrative personnel. Since campus-wide networks were not yet common, many users had to make a trip to the computer center in order to even find a computer to establish the connection with Cornell. There were often long delays while printed output from the sessions were spooled back to a central line printer.

Many users found that the steep learning curve and other difficulties outweighed any gains from using the model. The system began to fall into disuse, and the EFPM budget-planning model soon became obsolete when spreadsheets and desktop computers became popular. The technology had became an obstacle to the primary mission of sharing data.

The Booth Experiment. At a HEDS meeting (the membership organization that evolved out of the Tufts-Educom project), a daring but low-tech suggestion was made by David Booth of Williams College. Since all institutions had to complete the standard set of Higher Education General Information (HEGIS; later IPEDS) surveys, he suggested that the members simply photocopy the surveys and submit them to a central office. The HEDS staff soon took over the task of collecting the surveys, keying in the data, and preparing a final paper report with comparative data and simple summary statistics. A paper report was then mailed back to the members, along with a diskette containing a Lotus spreadsheet version of the data. Turnaround time from submission of the survey to receipt of the final report was generally two to three months.

This simple process succeeded where the high-tech solution had failed. It eliminated the need for each institutional representative to become a technical expert. Data-entry tasks were shifted to a more appropriate level, freeing institutional researchers to spend more time analyzing the data. Data transmission now relied primarily on the reliable (and universally accessible) technology of photocopy machines and the U.S. Postal Service. Participation in HEDS surveys by its then-current members dramatically increased, and many more institutions joined the organization. A low-technology solution had helped the organization reach the critical mass required to make the benefits of data sharing outweigh the costs of providing information.

Floppy Problems. Although the problem may seem trivial today, the distribution of data disks presented another case of developing technology interfering with ease of data access. There were major file translation obstacles across the various computer operating systems and different software products used by the membership. Most members used IBM-compatible computers, but others used Macintoshes. Several types and versions of spreadsheets were in use, and often these were incompatible with one another. Initially, all disks were distributed on 5¼ inch floppies in Lotus 1-2-3 format, and each institution was responsible for making any necessary conversions. Eventually, many members converted to desktop computers that had only 3½" floppy drives, or to Macintoshes, which could not then conveniently read DOS-formatted disks. Likewise, many members found it difficult to go through the multiple steps required to locate the software or hardware needed to transfer, translate, or convert files to a format usable in their own particular computing environment. Inconvenience once again interfered with utility.

The technical problem was again resolved using the HEDS staff resources. Rather than have each member go through the various steps needed to read the disks, the staff could more efficiently prepare customized disks in bulk at the central office. A "least common denominator" approach was taken to distribute data and disks. According to the individual needs of the members, data disks were prepared and distributed with files in either Macintosh or MS-DOS formats. Lotus, Excel, and plain text (ASCII) formats were adopted as common file standards because they could be opened by almost all spreadsheets. To ensure universality of access, HEDS files were and still are saved in formats used by older versions of the spreadsheets. When all else fails, tab-separated ASCII text remains the most basic "least common denominator" for universal access, but it is used as a last resort because some of the value added by the HEDS staff in the original reports may be lost (for example, formulas, text styles, and some layouts).

First Steps to the Net: The Response Is in the Mail. As electronic mail became available to more member institutions and institutional researchers in the late 1980s, HEDS established a BITNET LISTSERV mailing list for its members (Dunn, 1989). This LISTSERV is still actively used today. Any member with a general question about institutional policies, surveys, and the like can distribute a query to all members on the distribution list. Several simple surveys are conducted regularly over the mailing list, and turnaround time from data submission to final report is now usually measured in days rather than months. The mailing list also democratizes and decentralizes the process of data sharing because HEDS members will often conduct surveys that could not normally be done by the central HEDS staff. One member's annual electronic mail survey of numbers of admissions applications and deposits is a case in point. By providing a few simple figures, HEDS members get valuable feedback about the state of the current admissions pool almost immediately after the admissions deadlines arrive.

The HEDS list remains active today, with several queries distributed to the membership each week. One reason for the success of the mailing list is that a critical mass of the members have been, and are, frequent users of electronic mail. The Consortium's use of e-mail is an example of taking opportunistic advantage of a technology that developed independently of the membership. Similar lists can be used to meet the temporary communication needs of a working committee, of campus or regional organizations or interest groups, or even as a limited file distribution system. While electronic mail has been around in some form for many years, it took time for the technology to expand beyond the technical circles, to be demystified, and to become more user-friendly, generally available, and accepted in campus administrative offices.

File Servers. In the fall of 1992, HEDS took a further step in facilitating data exchange when the organization established a File Transfer Protocol (FTP) file server at its present offices at Franklin and Marshall College. All current and recent archival data files are now directly accessible to members through the Internet. The confidentiality of data and organizational data-sharing standards are preserved through a double security wall. Access to the FTP server is restricted rather than universal (for example, there is no "anonymous FTP"), and only HEDS members may log in with their institutional user ID and password. Furthermore, data files are stored in directories which provide "read permission" approval for only the institutions which actually submitted data for the file. The server also acts as a central location for posting administrative and membership information, storing a growing number of files which are too large to be distributed by floppy disk, and housing special files submitted by members. Among the advantages of the FTP server is the availability of time-critical data to members well in advance of the release of the final report, and the capacity to retrieve late surveys and corrections online at any time.

Unfortunately, the use of the file server is not without its difficulties. For instance, because there is still no simple and universal access method to the Internet shared by all institutions, providing technical instructions about how to connect to the file server can be complicated. Instructions vary according to the network gateway hardware or software being used by member institutions. Some members must connect to the file server by first connecting to their institution's network gateway mainframe computer, while others can connect directly from their desktop computers using TCP/IP technology. In addition, some members can download files with user-friendly, client-server software, such as Fetch or Anarchie, but others cannot. Procedures also vary depending upon whether members are users of Macintosh, MS-DOS, or Windows operating systems. While some HEDS members have volunteered to act as technical consultants for members having difficulty connecting to the server, some users with nonstandard computing environments may only be able to get technical support from their own campus computing centers.

Because some members still have limited network access in their offices, or come from institutions which do not provide full Internet access, the full paper report or floppy disk file distribution option is still available to everyone. Many members now download data files from the file server exclusively (saving the organization the cost of preparing and mailing disks). In times of technological transition, it is useful to make data available through multiple methods. Wherever possible, users should be able to obtain shared data by whatever means is most convenient. Therefore, data-sharing consortia need to strike a balance; individuals with limited access should not be left out, but those with more sophisticated technical capabilities should not be held back from using new technologies while others catch up.

Data Flow Both Ways. In the fall of 1994, HEDS took the next step in the automation of data sharing. Realizing that most of the members had the capability to *download* files, why not go a step further and *upload* the responses to the HEDS membership surveys as well? As an initial experiment, a small number of members were sent an extra copy of an annual survey on floppy disk. The survey appeared as a structured data-entry template in spreadsheet format, along with a sample copy of the original paper survey. The institution supplying the data had only to type in the responses in the appropriate columns or rows and upload a copy of the completed survey to the HEDS file server using FTP (or a client-server helper such as Fetch or Anarchie). While the survey could just as easily have been sent out in ASCII format as an e-mail message, the provision of a structured spreadsheet template gives the data collectors better control over the format and layout of the results. With a structured template laid out in spreadsheet format, each column or row represents a data element in a precise location. Thus, each institution's response can be entered into the master survey template by simply copying and pasting the column or row containing the institution's data into the master data file. As this experiment is extended to the general membership, it will not only help to limit postage expenses incurred by both the members and the central office, but it will also significantly reduce the amount of redundant data entry.

In one sense, HEDS is returning to its original goals (back in the EFPM and Cornell days) of submitting and retrieving data electronically. This time, however, the technology is not so much the obstacle, but the facilitator.

Emerging Technologies

The second part of this chapter goes beyond the experience of the HEDS Consortium to explore some new developments in technology that can facilitate data sharing both within and across institutions. Some of the examples discussed are well tested and already widely available; others still require a fairly high level of technical skill to use, but almost certainly will become the common methods for data exchange in the future.

Electronic Mail—Beyond ASCII. Electronic mail is too often used as simply a method for sending ASCII text back and forth across the network. Unfortunately, ASCII text is a very poor container for handling the types of files institutional researchers use every day. Text styles and formats are lost, columnar data may be mangled, graphics are not supported, and material is forced into an eighty-character line length. The need to "dumb-down" information sent in ASCII format so it appears as meaningful information at the receiver's end discourages the use of this mode of sharing data with colleagues.

Institutional researchers need the ability to exchange word processor documents, spreadsheets, tables, charts, and other files in *binary* or *image* format with clients and colleagues. Sending binary files through electronic mail has long been possible, but the technical hassles and steep learning curve involved have until recently made it impractical for most users.

Fortunately, many modern electronic mail systems now automate file translation and make it much easier to send binary files as attachments or enclosures to a normal electronic mail message. Improved desktop-to-mainframe interfaces are available so that a user never needs to connect manually to a mainframe to check mail. Client-server software (such as the popular Eudora mail package) will periodically and automatically connect from a desktop computer to the mainframe, download any mail messages found directly to the desktop, and notify the user that there are new messages.

Sending non-ASCII files as electronic mail attachments can be as simple as opening a directory window and pointing to the files on the desktop computer. The software converts the files into a commonly used transfer format (such as uuencode, binhex, MIME, or zip) and uploads them to the mainframe, which sends the files to their ultimate destination. If the recipient is using Eudora or a similar attachment-capable package, the software itself will convert and reconstruct the original file on the recipient's computer. Even large files of a megabyte or more can be transferred quickly and transparently.

The implications of adopting a good, user-friendly desktop electronic mail client cannot be overemphasized. Cooperative projects between institutional research colleagues are expedited when files can be rapidly shared. Preliminary results of surveys can be exchanged by electronic mail for proofreading. Many other efforts can be pursued as well. For instance, I cooperate with a colleague in another small institutional research office to produce custom internal peer group subset reports from HEDS survey results. Since we have very similar peer groups, we had been duplicating a lot of effort as we each produced our own summary reports for internal distribution. Now we often divide up responsibility for producing the internal summaries for various reports. The resulting draft Excel spreadsheets are exchanged using Eudora, and we each simply delete any nonshared peer institutions from our final reports. Our collaboration saves us both time and clerical work and makes the information available to both institutions much sooner than would otherwise be possible.

Gopher and the Web: Rodents and Arachnids in Cyberspace. In the past few years, the arrival of the World Wide Web and navigation aids such as Gopher and Netscape have revolutionized the way people use the Internet. These tools are responsible for much of the recent explosive growth of the Internet and extension of the so-called information superhighway to the general public. Gopher and World Wide Web clients intelligently automate many of the commands and integrate many of the software packages formerly needed to navigate the Internet. Before Gopher and the Web, full Internet access meant having to learn a constantly growing suite of access tools and protocols (such as FTP, archie, WAIS, and others). Gopher and WWW clients use short, behind the scenes scripts, or pointers, to enable them to locate files quickly without the need to invoke programs such as FTP or WAIS. Both systems may use helper applications or internal code to automatically transfer and convert files. They also minimize actual connection time to remote computers by eliminating human intervention and the need for users to enter cryptic commands.

Gopher was developed in 1991 at the University of Minnesota and was the first of the major user-friendly Internet navigation tools. Navigating through Gopherspace involves successively selecting a series of nested hierarchical menus to narrow down the search until the required information is found. Any item appearing in Gopherspace (text, pictures, data bases, directories, searchable items) will appear as a menu item.

The World Wide Web (WWW) system, developed by CERN (the European Laboratory for Particle Physics) takes an entirely different approach. While WWW information can be menu driven, the real advantage of the WWW is that it will treat any file or information as a hypertext link. Instead of tunneling through an endless series of structured menus, the WWW encourages random exploration by permitting jumps in any direction at any time. Just about any information can be linked to any other information, anywhere in the world.

The impact of these systems has profound implications for those who share and store large amounts of information. Gopher and Web systems provide, in effect, a bottomless hard drive to Internet users. Data residing anywhere on the planet can be quickly discovered and seamlessly downloaded so that they are virtually on the user's computer. The primary question is no longer that of *ownership* of files, but of being able to *access* them when they are needed.

Furthermore, Gopher and Web systems give institutional researchers the power to design and organize pointers to key information so that other campus information consumers can easily locate and read files which may have been buried on the Internet like needles in haystacks. HTML (Hypertext Markup Language) hypertext gives anyone the ability to design and publish a home page with a customized presentation of cyberspace. (See Appendix A at the end of this volume for more information on HTML hypertext.) Links to personal or organizational home pages can be "published" for all to see, or the path to a page can be kept private and made available only to a limited group.

Data sharing becomes simply a matter of informing others of the address (URL) of a home page, or posting a public link on the campus web. Since data can reside anywhere, this should encourage members of data-sharing consortia to take on decentralized research projects on behalf of the group.

Campus Wide Information Systems and Informal Data Sharing. As soon as Gopher and WWW systems reached a critical mass of users, institutions began to use these tools to develop Campus Wide Information Systems (CWIS). A CWIS turns any networked computer into an information kiosk. The CWIS may be centrally controlled by an official information provider (often the computer center or the publications office), or portions of it may be maintained by the individual offices which provide the data. Likewise, CWIS information may either be consolidated on a mainframe computer or distributed on a number of decentralized machines, often including desktop computers.

Any office can organize and publish a section of an institution's CWIS with only a few hours of technical training and a little practice. A variety of software utilities make writing the HTML code easy, and new releases of most major word processors now include HTML translators. Institutional researchers are discovering that the campus CWIS is an excellent way of distributing general college information to a variety of audiences. The number of online Web sites maintained by institutional research offices is rapidly growing. These range from basic ASCII text electronic factbooks to extremely sophisticated information systems with links to data archives or live mainframe data. By posting key institutional indicators online, the IR office can reduce the amount of time it spends responding to the common questions about enrollment, faculty size, and the like. Making available common sets of official institutional statistics will reduce confusion, and perhaps eventually reduce the time spent preparing the annual onslaught of college guidebook surveys. For example, the University of California at Irvine now places a common survey response on-line to publish all the statistics which are most commonly requested by college guidebooks and other outsiders.

To the extent that institutions are using their CWIS to publicly post statistical information about themselves, a new, informal, and somewhat chaotic (and perhaps dangerous) form of data sharing is taking place. Academic cyberspace is currently a technofrontier, where there are no common design standards, few accuracy checks, and where, unfortunately, the best advice to consumers of data obtained from publicly accessible sources is "let the buyer beware." Many institutions are aggressively using their CWIS as a marketing tool or a public relations device, and the accuracy of published data may suffer as a result. Some campus sites contain data that are outdated or simply erroneous. However, once posted, unless special security steps have been implemented, the information becomes available throughout the Internet for anyone to discover and will remain there indefinitely. Institutional researchers should be aware of just what information about an institution can be discovered on the Internet, who can access it, and how accurate it is. They should also educate others on campus about the implications of data sharing on the Web, for good or for bad.

In another sense, the opportunity to decide whether or not to share information is being taken out of the hands of colleges and universities. Institutions release a considerable amount of information about themselves to government or private surveys which may end up on the Internet, with or without an institution's knowledge or permission. Governmental and private organizations that collect national educational data are making them more readily available on the Web, and the information can often be viewed at the level of an individual institution. For example, in New York state, the Department of Education has collected and summarized the data gathered for IPEDS and its own statewide surveys. Anyone can now go to the NYSED gopher and download a neat longitudinal summary of any public or private institution's admissions, enrollment, or financial statistics for the past several years. The state has added real value to the data by compiling and organizing the annual survey responses.

Easily accessible data may be an information bonanza for institutional researchers, but such data may also be a source of concern for administrators who realize that competitors now have a free, ready-made, and intimate view of the data history of their institutions. The U.S. Department of Education already makes available much of the raw data from the IPEDS series on its servers, and it is investigating ways to place IPEDS data into a Structured Query Language (SQL) data base for Internet access. The Association of American University Professors' (AAUP) faculty salary statistics have been published on-line by the *Chronicle of Higher Education*. Anyone who can locate the information can download it. The major problem is that many public sources take about a year to post the current survey results.

The commercial value of networked data about academic institutions has been discovered and exploited. Most of the major college guidebook companies have established Web servers, and some are publishing the information from their guidebook surveys either on the WWW or on CD-Rom. The Peterson's Education Center web publishes just a few basic statistics about participating institutions (after all, who would buy the guidebooks if the contents were available on the Web for free?) In contrast, the Princeton Review has posted most of the results of its recent survey of its so-called top 306 institutions. The Princeton Review site should be of great interest and concern to colleges, since it contains not only the statistical data provided by the colleges themselves, but the results of its own independent surveys of students' attitudes about selected campuses. The institutional profiles of selected institutions draw heavily on student quotes, and many of the published quotes seem to have been chosen by the Review editors for their outrageousness or for their sensational claims about the colleges. Furthermore, the Princeton Review site contains a series of dubious Top 20 lists that claim to rate colleges and universities in categories such as "the students (almost) never study," "students pray/ignore God on a regular basis," "lots of hard liquor," etc. The methodology used to produce the lists is never explained, but their publication is sure to make admissions deans cringe. Colleges and universities that feel they have been unfairly portrayed have no way of countering or challenging the bad publicity.

Under the present state of affairs, locating a specific data element on the Web about a specific institution is very much a hit-or-miss operation, requiring some skill and a good bit of luck. Net surfers need to take care to consider the source, quality, and timeliness of the data they find. Individual institutional research offices need to take a more aggressive role in seeing that the electronically published information about their institutions is accurate and organized in a coherent fashion.

The proliferation of governmental and commercial Internet sites should not be a vital threat to existing data-sharing consortia, but they will need to adapt to changing times. Data-sharing consortia can help train institutional researchers to publish their own data, and can perhaps establish some common format or standard presentation guidelines for Net-published material. Consortia have special expertise in making information available in a timely fashion, whereas commercial and governmental data are often out of date before they are published. If proper security precautions are taken, consortia should be able to further reduce the turnaround time from initial data submission to the distribution of final reports. As concerns about the accuracy of published public institutional statistics rise, data-sharing consortia may lobby on behalf of their members to encourage commercial Web sites to use current statistics and not to publish misleading information. Data-sharing groups will want to establish Web pages for members and make use of new and more user-friendly ways to allow members to access their data archives.

Campus Wide Information Systems and Online Electronic Factbooks: Points to Consider. The new Internet presentation tools give institutional researchers the ability to design a "customized view of the world" or a "universe in a shoebox" to guide users on campus, or to carefully "package" the types of campus information that will be seen by off-campus users. Any IR office can design a system to organize and give the public full access to the data bases of the Bureau of the Census, key financial indicators, IPEDS data, and the archives of the Electronic AIR.

Setting up an online electronic factbook may be more difficult to do from a bureaucratic and political perspective than from a technical one. Before attempting such a project, the institutional researcher should have authorization from appropriate administrators and a clear sense of what information the institution is willing to share, and with what audience it is willing to share it. Receiving authorization to proceed with the project will undoubtedly require that some fundamental questions are first answered:

1. *Who are the users?* When designing a CWIS, it is important to consider both the audience and the scope of the information. Is it expected to be a resource for key administrators? If so, are the people most likely to need the resource comfortable enough with computers and the CWIS to actually use online data? Is the factbook intended to be a public information source for the campus community? If so, an online factbook is an ideal way of reducing the

expense of printing and distributing paper factbooks. Are public terminals available for maintenance and service staff who do not normally have access to computers? Is the CWIS intended as a public relations tool to communicate with alumni, potential students, or the Internet world as a whole? As technology improves, a state of the art CWIS can even interact securely with administrative mainframes to automate many of the routine clerical and administrative transactions of a campus. For example, the University of Delaware has recently implemented a very extensive web-based information system which allows students and staff to get transcripts, pay bills, check their status, apply for admission, prepare management reports, and much more (Wilson, 1995). The intended audience will largely determine (or restrict) what should go into the factbook.

2. *What security and access restrictions will be employed (if any)?* The security of information should always be a key concern; Gopher and WWW systems can be configured so that access is restricted only to on-campus use, or so that information is available to the entire Internet community. WWW servers can be configured so that access is restricted by password to a limited set of individuals. However, even when a file server is password-protected, the data provider needs to be extremely meticulous to keep information secure from hackers. Special care should be taken to ensure that appropriate users of files and directories are given the proper access privileges, and that the security of files are tested from both on and off campus. Extremely sensitive information may not be appropriate for posting on a campus web; if the goal is to establish an Executive Information System (EIS), a secure file server protected from outside access by a "firewall" may be a better alternative. In any case, consultations with the campus network security expert are essential.

3. *Who owns the information?* Unless the institution has a relatively open information policy, and that policy is made clear to all, an on-line factbook may cause interoffice turf wars or attempts to micromanage or sugar-coat what is posted. Some administrators may object to having any detailed institutional information made available on-line; others may want to post sensitive information freely without fully realizing that it may reach the wrong audience. Either way, a process of education is necessary; administrators may want to restrict access because they may not be aware of the extent to which internal information is already available from published sources. When several offices maintain portions of the CWIS, the chance that inconsistent data will be published grows. Institutional researchers should provide the necessary oversight to ensure that published numbers are in fact the official numbers that represent the institution.

Many campuses have set up committees to discuss issues of access and ownership concerning electronic information. Written policies should clearly define guidelines for which types of information may be posted and which may not. It may help to have senior administrators and those posting the data sign an information sponsors' agreement specifying which types of information may be posted, and which offices or individuals are authorized to do so. Parts of a

CWIS may be designated as official campus documents and be strictly monitored for content and accuracy, whereas other portions may be left unsupervised to encourage designers to explore the creativity and experimentation that has come to typify the Internet revolution. Safeguards should always be taken to ensure that privacy and license rights and copyrights are protected. Some campus information that would normally be considered public takes on a different dimension when made available on the Internet. For example, it might be appropriate to post home phones or addresses in a limited-distribution paper campus directory; however, posting that information in an electronic format available on the Internet might be inadvisable, and in some cases might even pose a security risk to those listed in the directory.

4. *Who maintains the information and how?* It is important to have a campus information providers' agreement that explicitly lays out the responsibilities and duties of those authorized to post information on the CWIS. In general, information is most reliable when it is posted by those who generate it. However, this is not always practical, because the primary information providers may be too busy, lack the needed technical skills, or fail to understand or accept the mission of a CWIS. The institutional research office can take the lead to gather, consolidate, and refine the core set of data to be made available as an electronic factbook. In some cases, publishing an on-line factbook as a demonstration project may be all that is needed to convince other offices of the potential value of a full-scale campus information system. Whoever ultimately is charged with posting the information should also have the responsibility of making sure that it is kept up-to-date. A common guideline is to post the last revision date, the name of the information provider, and the URL of the page at the bottom of each page in the CWIS.

5. *What design standards are adopted?* Graphic standards and style issues are another factor to consider. Often, the publications office may issue strict guidelines about the look and feel of institutional publications. Restrictions may be placed on the use of the institutional logo, or certain page layout standards may be imposed. Publications guidelines may be difficult to define and enforce in the ever-changing world of electronic publications, but it is still important that there be an overall sense of consistency and unity in the official portion of a CWIS.

6. *How should the files be stored?* One of the most frustrating problems caused by the rapid transformation of the Internet is the challenge of achieving an appropriate balance so that documents will reach the intended audience in an attractive manner and in a way that takes advantage of the best of recent technological developments. Some alternative options for making information available are explored below.

a. *ASCII text:* Plain text is still the "least common denominator" method to ensure nearly universal access. It is still the only easy way to display gopher-based information. Many dial-in network users will be limited to text-based terminals. However, formatting tabular institutional research information so that it will display properly on a text-based terminal can be tedious and frustrating, and the on-screen results are less than attractive. Table columns must be carefully lined up using monospaced fonts. Even then, tables may still not display properly on the user's screen because some commercial on-line services use proportional fonts in their default browsers.

b. *HTML markup:* Producing basic hypertext markup language documents is not as difficult as it sounds, and numerous public domain or shareware editors are available. HTML macros are also available as add-ins to the most popular word processors. Although text may be neatly displayed with various style formats (boldface, italics), data tables can be a problem because HTML collapses groups of empty spaces between text. This problem can be overcome by surrounding a table with the HTML preformatted text style codes (<pre> and </pre>), but it will still appear as an unattractive plain ASCII table. A very attractive HTML "tables" format has been developed, but the codes are somewhat complicated, and many older and text-based Web browsers will not display the tables properly. The popular Netscape Web browser uses extensions to the standard HTML codes and although Netscape-enhanced documents look spectacular, they don't always display properly through other Web browsers.

c. *GIF files:* A GIF (Graphics Interchange Format) file is a standard graphics file format that can be displayed by all desktop computers' graphics-capable Gopher and Web browsers. Rather than go through the steps to convert tables into clean ASCII text, some electronic factbook designers simply take a screen snapshot of tables in their production spreadsheets, convert them to GIF images, and include the images as links to a hypertext document. Using tables and charts published in GIF image format will reduce the need to produce separate versions of the same information for the factbook and for paper copies. Although this method is quick, some drawbacks are that the image files may be large, they may take a long time to display, and the images of text tables may not print with laser printer quality. End users will not be able to cut and paste data from the tables into other applications because the tables are now bit-mapped images rather than text characters. Users of text-based Web browsers such as Lynx won't be able to directly display the images, although the images can be downloaded and viewed on a desktop computer. Those who access the CWIS by modem or with Web browsers on commercial services may not appreciate the extra time required to download pages with extensive graphics.

d. *Standard file formats:* If a campus has adopted and supports a standard set of software packages (for example, they support only DOS or only Macintosh formats, or within a given format they only support WordPerfect or MS Word word processors, or Excel or Lotus spreadsheets), files may be posted directly to the Gopher or Web server as documents saved in the formats and packages common to the campus. Common formats will allow end users to work directly with original files and will reduce the effort needed to write complicated HTML pages. The files can be transferred to a desktop, or the browser can be configured to directly launch the application. Some organizations have used this method to distribute Excel spreadsheets containing (sanitized) raw data along with predefined DataPivot tables and charts. With some basic instruction, end users can interact with the pivot tables to explore all aspects of the data and ultimately to produce and print their own reports.

In institutions where there are no standard software packages, another option is to save and post documents in the Adobe Acrobat .pdf (portable document file) format. With the aid of a freely distributable reader application or Netscape plug-in, these files will display properly on any major desktop computer. Since it is unlikely that any single method will be suitable to everyone, ASCII and non-ASCII alternative versions should be provided whenever possible. The Data and Planning Support office at the University of Arizona tries to reach the widest possible audience by posting many of its factbook files in ASCII, Excel, Lotus, and Adobe .pdf formats.

With a little study, any institutional research office or data-sharing consortium should be able to provide a basic Web page containing information about the institution or its members. Some systems may have elaborate graphics and button-driven user interfaces; others may offer just the basic data. Some institutions have sophisticated data systems that will automatically download and update on-line data; most small institutions will only be able to update a simple electronic factbook on an annual basis. As with any data sharing, the key is to know the audience, their technical capabilities or limitations, and their hardware and software environments.

Next Technologies: Interactive and Real-Time Data Sharing. The technology of the Web is, to borrow a phrase from the creators of Mosaic, changing as rapidly as time. Inevitably much of the content of this chapter will be out of date by the time it is published. But it is possible to speculate in what direction we are headed based on some of the utilities that are now being perfected (Thomas, 1995).

1. *Interactive forms and scripts.* Most Web browsers have support for interactive forms, which allow the end user to retrieve or post information to or from a remote information server. A form consists of a number of text blocks, buttons, check boxes, and so forth that allow the end user to submit textual information, search requests, and other feedback back to the Web server. Customized forms may be designed for almost any purpose, and with almost any level of complexity. The most common forms provide data-entry text blocks to request simple information (such as the user's name and address) and to send it in one direction—to the Web page owner's data base. With a little work, institutional researchers and data-sharing consortia can use HTML forms to conduct some of their multiple-response or free-response surveys on the Web. By eliminating paper surveys and submitting data in electronic form, there is less need for redundant data entry. When HTML forms are linked to other software or scripts, they can serve as the user interface to sophisticated data bases, or provide a very user-friendly front end for data entry, queries, or other interactions. HTML forms may someday vindicate the old HEDS EFPM data submission experiments.

A number of freely-distributable tools can be installed in campus mainframes that will make two-way interactive Web-based communication available to anyone without the need for extensive technical support or complicated programming. For example, Common Gateway Interface (CGI) scripts are add-in utilities that allow Web servers to execute custom commands based on user input. One such program, cgiemail, takes HTML form input, sends it through ordinary e-mail, and filters the output to automate a number of clerical tasks. Cgiemail uses a data layout template, written as a companion to the original form, to determine how the submitted data fields will appear to the person (or machine) who receives the submitted form.

As a hypothetical example, suppose a college uses a Web-based data-entry form to submit a survey to its data-sharing consortium. The message goes through the mail and is interpreted by cgiemail or a similar program. Behind the scenes, the field values are manipulated, redirected, recycled, rearranged, and filtered for a variety of purposes. Plain copies of the survey are automatically mailed to the relevant employees for archiving. A personalized receipt or thank you letter is automatically mailed back to the submitter along with a summary of the submitted data so that they can be checked for errors. In another action, the submitted data elements are rearranged so that they can be imported into a spreadsheet or data base for further analysis. At the same time, the data elements are converted into HTML script so they may be posted on the consortium's Web server (in a password-protected area, open only to members). All of the data entry was done once by the person sending the form.

Many institutions are already using interactive forms to submit direct queries to live data on administrative mainframes, to interact with library catalogs, and much more.

2. *Personal agents.* As artificial intelligence technology improves, computers will start to learn our routines and our daily needs. They will become more like personal secretaries or agents, searching for the information we need when we need it. CRAYON (CReAte Your Own Newspaper) is an interesting example of this potential using only low-tech HTML forms. Suppose that each morning one wants to read a world news summary, check out the latest EDUPAGE newsletter, view a regional satellite weather map, and check the latest Dow Jones average. Gathering all the information would require taking an extensive tour around the Internet. However, the CRAYON page first asks you what you want to read, and in what order you care to have it presented. Once the form is submitted, CRAYON generates HTML links to gather the information from numerous public sites all over the Internet. The responses are compiled and delivered as a personalized daily electronic newspaper with only the news items requested. A CRAYON-like system could be configured to meet more specialized information needs of institutional researchers. Other more sophisticated software, such as WAIS (Wide Area Information Server) can periodically or continuously monitor an Internet archive for information on specified topics and notify you when it finds a relevant item or when new matches arrive. Imagine arriving at work in the morning and being notified by your

computer agent that the latest AAUP faculty salary report is finally available on the data-consortium file server and that the latest notice of proposed rule making on the Student Right-to-Know Act has finally appeared in the Federal register. Then imagine the agent offering to download it for you immediately.

3. *Teleconferencing and Telepresence.* Conferences, committee meetings, and a variety of other collaborative activities are best conducted face-to-face or by phone, but travel and conference calls are expensive. A number of free or low-cost tools are available or are under development to make teleconferencing available through the Internet. The popular Internet Relay Chat (IRC) is a multi-user implementation of the old UNIX talk program. It is perhaps best described as the Internet equivalent of citizen's band radio, although conversations are text based. Several people can simultaneously participate in a discussion over a particular channel, or even multiple channels. Anyone can create a new channel and there is no restriction on the number of people who can participate in a discussion in real time. Files can even be transferred from person to person while a discussion takes place. Some newer text-based conferencing systems allow users to represent themselves graphically using icons, cartoons, or even photographs. For example, CompuServe has opened the WorldsAway Community Forum conferencing system which allows members to be represented by customized characters (called *avatars*) who can meet and walk around in virtual rooms, make gestures and change expressions, manipulate virtual objects, and even furnish virtual apartments in a cartoon-like cyberspace.

RealAudio *audio on demand* software allows one-way distribution of lengthy audio programs over the Internet in real time. With this or similar software, people who are unable to attend national conferences can select and listen to digital "tapes" of conference proceedings at their convenience in their own offices. Two-way live communication is now possible with the commercial NetPhone software. NetPhone allows users to conduct live conversations by computer through a network or with a 14.4K baud modem without paying long-distance charges. (Both parties must have the software and a computer microphone.) Cornell University's CU-See Me software is the first product to allow live multiparty videoconferencing on the Internet to users with the software, a desktop video camera, and a video digitizing board. Image quality is not high, and the program is a heavy user of network resources, but the product may become more practical for general audiences in the future. Higher-bandwidth full-motion video transmission over the Internet is still at the experimental stage.

4. *Getting wired beyond the network.* Until recently, Internet access from a home office meant dialing in to the campus network by modem. While most Internet tools are available by this method, they have been limited to the ASCII-based terminal (and often user-hostile) versions. Only a fraction of the multimedia advances on the WWW are available using text-based mainframe web browsers such as Lynx. New services such as SLIP (Serial Line Internet Protocol), PPP (Point to Point Protocol), and TIA (The Internet Adaptor) allow

full Internet access using familiar client-server software. SLIP and PPP require that the institution set up a special server to handle these connections. Researchers can check with the computer support staff to see if the service is available at their institutions. If not, SLIP or PPP access might be available for a fee from a local commercial Internet service provider. TIA is a commercial product that allows access to client-server tools directly from a user's UNIX account in cases where SLIP and PPP are not available. Many commercial services, such as CompuServe, Prodigy, and America OnLine are beginning to offer limited Internet access services to their subscribers (Crotty and Pearlstein, 1995).

All of these services still require connection via modem, and the higher the baud rate, the better. A 9600 or 14400 baud modem are probably the minimum speeds at which dial-in service will function acceptably. Even at these speeds, access to WWW services that rely heavily on multimedia may be painfully slow. Text-based access using mainframe-based tools may be preferable when speed is required.

Conclusion

Technology can be both an obstacle and a boon to cooperative data sharing within and across institutions. Taking an approach to data sharing that is too high-tech before a technology is ripe for general use by laypeople can be counterproductive. A low-tech approach may be more efficient when general access to emerging technologies is limited, or when the learning curve is too steep. Until recently, there have been formidable obstacles to transferring compatible data across varieties of mainframe and desktop computers, or across different operating systems and software packages. People who wish to share information widely have been limited by their colleagues' varying levels of access to, and understanding of, network and hardware technology. Technophobia, lack of information, budget constraints, or lack of appropriate hardware, software, or network access all pose obstacles to making the best use of available technology. Taking the least common denominator approach provides the most information to the largest number of individuals, but it also can mean being constrained by the needs of the weakest links in the technological chain and forgoing advances that are available to growing numbers of institutional researchers. Whenever possible, alternative methods of access to data should be provided to promote their wider distribution. Sometimes taking a state-of-the-art approach is well worth the effort in spite of the additional learning burden it places on the designers, because the end result will be that more information actually gets shared and used. The explosion of campus-wide information systems is a prime example of how the availability of a user-friendly interface can completely change the way people work.

Many technical difficulties can be overcome by encouraging the staff of data-sharing consortia to take the lead in promoting new methods of access to information and by providing more education and technical support for the membership. Existing data-sharing consortia will face growing competition as more and more data can be gathered from CWIS systems and government and private information brokers. Consortia staff can respond to this competition by providing new services tailored to meet the specific needs of their members. Customized peer reports, direct query access to data base archives, more longitudinal studies, and providing information on demand are services they should consider providing. In a chaotic information environment, existing data-sharing groups should take the lead to establish rational standards for timely and orderly collection, presentation, and distribution of information. They can promote the use of electronically published standard survey response formats to reduce the confusion and the amount of time wasted filling out a proliferation of for-profit guidebook surveys. As always, they need to understand the technical capabilities and information needs of their members, and to recognize when the time for a new technology has come.

References

Crotty, C., and Pearlstein, J. "Make the Right Connection." *MacWorld,* Oct. 1995, 104–109.

Dunn, J. A., Jr. "Electronic Media and Information Sharing." In P. T. Ewell (ed.), *Enhancing Information Use in Decision Making.* New Directions for Institutional Research, no. 64. San Francisco: Jossey-Bass, 1989, 73–84.

Thomas, C. R. "Harnessing Information Technology in the Twenty-First Century." In T. R. Sanford (ed.), *Preparing for the Information Needs of the Twenty-First Century.* New Directions for Institutional Research, no. 85. San Francisco: Jossey-Bass, 1995, 65–74.

Wilson, D. L. "Extending the Web: University of Delaware Decides to Use Internet Tool for Most Routine Business." *Chronicle of Higher Education,* Aug. 11, 1995, A17.

JAMES C. FERGERSON is director of Institutional Research at Bates College in Lewiston, Maine. He can be reached over the Internet at his IR home page at URL: http://www.bates.edu/IR/IR.html

Prior to joining a data-sharing organization, potential participants need to address a series of questions regarding their goals and expectations for engaging in such an activity.

Coming Aboard: Making the Decision to Join a Data-Sharing Organization

James F. Trainer

Each of the preceding chapters in this volume provided insight into a particular aspect of participating in an inter-institutional data exchange. The chapters covered such topics as guidelines for participating in data exchanges, the benefits and costs associated with engaging in such activities, and the technology involved in sharing data across institutions. Building on the information shared by the volume's other authors, this final chapter is designed to help individual readers decide whether joining a data-sharing group may prove beneficial to their institution. A series of questions are posed that those contemplating participating in data sharing should address prior to reaching a final decision on whether to participate in an exchange of any sort. Each of these questions is accompanied either by examples of the types of products one can expect to receive from a data-sharing activity or by a list of additional resources, beyond the scope of this volume, that the researcher may want to consult when making a decision about joining a data exchange.

Questions to Pursue

1. *Why do I need comparative data?* As noted in earlier chapters in this volume, there are many reasons why an institution might benefit from having comparative information. These include, among other things, having the ability to assess the institution's status relative to other institutions on such measures of institutional well-being as revenue streams and expenditure patterns and admission, retention, and graduation rates; being able to respond to calls from internal and external constituencies to benchmark an institution's practices and procedures against those of other institutions, and identifying and

understanding an institution's niche in the marketplace, whether for recruiting and attracting students, hiring faculty, or soliciting and receiving philanthropic gifts or research grants. Middaugh (1990) has suggested that institutional researchers need to collect and analyze input, process, and output data. All three of these types of data are useful in making inter-institutional comparisons. It is important, however, that prior to investing time and resources in compiling comparative data, the reasons for collecting such information are clearly understood. Choosing to pursue comparative data without a clear goal in mind may prove to be a wasteful decision. Institutions already warehouse much information that is rarely or never used; there is no need to add to this excess volume unnecessarily.

2. *What types of information do I need?* The ultimate goal of any data collection and analysis enterprise in institutional research is to inform the decision-making process and to address questions such as, How are we doing as an institution? and, What can we do to improve our institutional operation and outcomes? Of course, these questions can be asked about any number of programs or operations. Thus, it may be helpful to think about the various aspects and activities of the institution as a way of determining what types of comparative information are needed to address the questions at hand. The organization of Russell and Rodriguez's (1993) *Compendium of National Data Sources on Higher Education* may prove useful in thinking about the various segments of an organization that might be examined. In addition to general references, their listings include information on student participation in higher education, finance and management issues, topics related to faculty, staffing and salaries, and factors such as physical facilities, libraries, and institutional assets. Each of these broad categories can be subdivided into numerous discrete topics:

Student participation
Admissions
Enrollments
Student characteristics
Retention
Degree completions
Satisfaction studies
Alumni follow-up studies

Faculty, staffing, and salaries
Faculty salaries
Administrative salaries
Faculty characteristics
Staffing patterns
Hiring practices
Fringe benefits
Productivity measures
Promotion and tenure rates

Finance and management
Tuition revenues
Public support
Voluntary support
Endowment support
Research grants and contracts
Financial aid
General expenditure patterns

Facilities, libraries, and assets
Research facilities
Overhead costs
Library holdings and statistics

In addition to the Russell and Rodriguez categories, the list of the National Center for Educational Statistics' (NCES) Integrated Postsecondary Education Data System (IPEDS) surveys is a good place to begin in thinking about the types of data that might be useful in making inter-institutional comparisons. The IPEDS survey series includes studies on institutional characteristics, fall enrollments, student tuition and fees, degree completions, salary, tenure and fringe benefits of faculty, financial statistics, academic libraries, and institutional staff. The data collected in these surveys often form the backbone of a data-sharing activity. Other efforts by NCES, such as the Recent College Graduates Study, the National Postsecondary Student Aid Study, and the Survey of Earned Doctorates Awarded in the United States, also provide clues to the types of information that might be useful to examine in comparing one's institution to others.

3. *What comparisons do I want to make?* The response to this question is multidimensional. First, decide the level at which you want to make your comparisons. Do you want to compare your institution with national data aggregated across all institutions regardless of their location and type? Or, do you want to restrict your comparative analyses to a certain type and size of institution? Do you want to draw comparisons with a specific group of institutions? Or, do you want to make a series of comparisons that represent some combination of the above? More than likely, you probably want to be able to make comparisons at a variety of levels.

In making comparisons with all institutions nationally or with all institutions nationally within a certain type (for example, public or private, four-year or two-year, baccalaureate, master's, or doctoral degree-granting), data from NCES may prove extremely useful, especially if you can access the data electronically either through NCES's FTP or Web sites or through the Quantum Research Corporation's Computer-Aided Science Policy Analysis and Research (CASPAR) data base. These sources also can be used to obtain information to make comparisons within a given state or region (see Chapter Five and Appendix A in this volume for additional information on accessing these data sites).

Unfortunately, the NCES and CASPAR data sources are not without their problems. Generally, the data may be older than one would like to have to inform decisions in what has become an increasingly rapidly-changing environment. In addition, these data bases are restricted to those that the NCES (and in the case of CASPAR, the National Science Foundation as well) collects and may fail to contain data that an institutional researcher or planner may need for a particular analysis. Finally, these data bases cover the universe of institutions in the United States and thus may require a good bit of work on the part of the individual researcher to extract only those data that come from institutions of particular interest.

Some of the difficulties cited above regarding the use of national data bases may be overcome by accessing data either by state (especially in those states that coordinate the collection of IPEDS data from the institutions within their state and make the data available sooner than they would be nationally (for instance, New York's Department of Education server), or from national or regional organizations of particular types of institutions (such as the Pennsylvania Independent College and University Research Center's exchange of IPEDS finance data). (Consult Russell's *Advances in Statewide Higher Education Data Systems* (1995) for more information on data, especially unit record data, at the statewide level.) Using data bases defined by state or institutional type can be more efficient than using national sources if the data are available sooner than they would be through broad national efforts, and if they help eliminate data that are not of any particular interest. Individual institutions, however, may want to make comparisons in a timely fashion with a group that is defined in some way other than just by location or type. For instance, although a liberal arts college that attracts students from a national pool may have some elements in common with other, more regional institutions in the state where it is located, it is more than likely that the most meaningful comparisons for that particular college would be made with similar institutions nationwide; thus planners at this liberal arts college may look for ways to make comparisons with similar institutions nationally without having to wait for or wade through NCES's IPEDS files. Such convenience and timeliness are major benefits of participation in a cooperative inter-institutional data exchange. The bottom line is that institutions need to draw comparisons on various levels. How these comparisons are made and the currency of the data used in the comparisons depend on the level at which the comparisons are drawn.

Beyond choosing the level at which comparisons are to be made, one must also decide what specific types of comparisons will be made. Will only raw data be compared? Will ratio analyses be conducted? Will the comparisons represent only single year snapshots or will they be longitudinal in nature? Will individual analyses be restricted to one given area, such as financial figures, or will analyses be more comprehensive, drawing data from across different aspects of the institution (for example, using data from fall enrollment and staff surveys along with financial data to calculate various per–full-time-equivalent (FTE) student or faculty ratios)? These are critical questions and the types of comparisons that one can draw depend on how these questions are answered. Needless to say, and depending on the responses to these questions, the analyses that can be conducted run the gamut from the simple to the complex. The reader interested in conducting the more complex analyses would be wise to consult Brinkman's *Conducting Interinstitutional Comparisons* (1987), as well as some of the other resources listed in Appendix B of this volume.

4. *How do I select specific institutions for comparisons?* A variety of institutional characteristics can be taken into consideration in choosing specific institutions with which to draw comparisons. Some of these characteristics, such as size, mission, Carnegie type, type of control, tradition, and geographic location are referenced in earlier sections of this chapter, as well as in earlier chapters in this volume (see specifically Chapters One and Two). However, the selection of an appropriate set of comparison institutions need not be restricted to a simple listing of institutions with common characteristics. The selection

of comparison institutions can be data driven. Numerous methodologies have been developed to guide the researcher in selecting an appropriate set of institutions for making valid inter-institutional comparisons. The work of Paul Brinkman and various associates (Brinkman, 1987; Brinkman & Teeter, 1987; and Brinkman & Krakower, 1983), Deborah Teeter and associates (Teeter, 1983; Teeter & Brinkman, 1992; and Teeter & Christal, 1987), and Patrick Terenzini (Terenzini, Hartmark, Lorang, and Shirley, 1980) should prove useful in helping researchers identify methods to use in selecting institutions for use in making inter-institutional comparisons. Many institutions will maintain multiple lists of comparison institutions. These lists may include traditional comparison lists as well as lists of institutions that institutional leadership aspires to emulate—these latter lists are often called *aspirant groups*. Some lists may be developed using traditional measures; others may be constructed using more complex methodologies.

5. *What data are accessible to me?* Institutions collect, maintain, analyze, and submit to various entities a plethora of institutional information. Data seem to be a natural byproduct of the normal functioning of institutions. Nearly every institutional function produces data of some sort. Many of these data—admissions, financial aid and enrollment statistics, finance and personnel figures, course registrations, grades and evaluations, degree and certificate completion counts—are familiar to most readers. In fact, many institutional researchers have ready access to this information for their individual institutions. Researchers may also have access to data from student, faculty, alumni, and community surveys.

Theoretically, all of the aforementioned data could be employed in making inter-institutional comparisons. If your institution collects and maintains certain data, it is likely that other institutions collect and maintain at least some of these data as well. One needs to think, however, how these data are collected and maintained on one's own campus, and where and to whom they are submitted externally, in order to gain a sense of whether these data would be readily available from other institutions for the sake of making comparisons. Certainly, we know that all data submitted as part of the IPEDS series will eventually be used that way. Likewise, the American Association of University Professors' (AAUP) annual faculty compensation data, the Council For Aid to Education's (CFAE) voluntary support data, and the National Association of College and University Business Officers' (NACUBO) endowment performance data are all available for sale to the public at the individual institutional level, albeit some of them encoded. Researchers can also access normative data, as well as their own institution's data, for such projects as the Cooperative Institutional Research Program's (CIRP) Freshmen and College Student Surveys and the College Student Experiences Questionnaire. Data from studies conducted by many other organizations are available as well (some of these are listed in Appendix B of this volume). A comprehensive list of data sources of all types is available in Russell and Rodriguez (1993). In addition, formally organized data-sharing organizations may create surveys to collect data in areas where members feel there is a need for inter-institutional data that is not already met through other sources. These organizations may also make arrangements to share data before they are released by other collecting agencies or to provide access to codes for unmasking encoded institutional data.

6. *How much time will this activity require?* The amount of time individual participants invest in data-sharing activities varies greatly, depending on the extent to which they are involved in the activity and how comprehensive the research agenda is for their institution or for the data-sharing group to which they belong. Some data exchanges have a singular focus and require very little time (or time once a year), whereas other organizations have extensive data-collection schedules that require a significant time commitment and consistent participation throughout the year. Some activities involve only making and sending out copies of existing forms, such as IPEDS surveys, whereas others require the development and maintenance of special-unit record-level electronic data files. As with most activities, one can only get out of the data-sharing activity what one is able to invest in it. Fortunately, most data exchanges allow members to pick and choose how and when they are going to participate, limiting access to data to only those institutions that have taken the time to submit the data. Within the Higher Education Data Sharing Consortium (HEDS), a comprehensive, formally organized data exchange conducting approximately twenty different projects a year, some institutional representatives are concerned that participation in the organization is too time consuming; however, other representatives cite the efficiency of the organization (in terms of what an institution receives in exchange for the time it commits to HEDS) as one of the Consortium's greatest strengths.

7. *What are the financial costs of participating in a data exchange?* Data-sharing activities vary both in their costs and how their costs are structured. Some activities, such as an informally organized exchange with a limited scope and onetime (or sporadic) data-submission schedule, may actually involve no direct financial cost to participating institutions and may rely solely on the voluntary goodwill of a participating member or members to develop and coordinate the exchange. Other data-sharing activities may be offshoots of existing organizations and their costs may be incorporated into the organization's membership fee. Still other organizations, such as HEDS, maintain offices and employ full-time staffs for the sole purpose of sharing data. Groups in this latter category generally collect an annual fee to cover the costs of central office operations and a predetermined set of standard projects. Activities beyond these projects are covered by supplemental fees paid by those institutions desiring and participating in these additional efforts. Fees for groups that are formally organized are generally set by a board of directors or some other formal decision-making body. In addition to regular membership fees and fees for supplemental projects, organizations may also collect registration fees if they host conferences. Given that data exchanges are member-driven organizations, the policies of these organizations are most often set by the members themselves. Every effort is generally made to keep the costs of membership to a minimum.

Between the cost-free and comprehensive fee organizations are those efforts that collect fees on a per-study basis—an arrangement that may be appealing to institutions interested in participating in relatively few studies on an ad hoc basis. Over time, however, the costs for these types of efforts build up, especially if an institution is not purposeful in deciding which activities it is going to engage in. In such cases, belonging to an organization with a comprehensive fee may prove to be a fiscally prudent route to pursue.

8. *How much technical expertise is required in order to share data?* As Jim Fergerson pointed out in Chapter Five of this volume, the technology involved in sharing data across institutions runs the gamut, from simply copying IPEDS forms and sending them to colleagues at other institutions, to using and creating very specific and sophisticated electronic data files and down- and uploading them to various FTP and Web sites. Most data sharing, however, requires only that you have a microcomputer tied to the Internet and that you are comfortable using standard spreadsheet and statistical software packages. If you lack an Internet connection, data can still be made available to you most of the time on diskette in standard spreadsheet or text formats. The only limiting factor to the approach of sharing data on diskette is that on occasion files may be larger than the capacity a diskette can accommodate. Fortunately, it seems that most individuals who coordinate data-sharing activities are accustomed to working in environments where tasks or files must be designed so they can be used by individuals using a variety of hardware configurations and software packages. Likewise, it is fortunate that many of the individuals who are employed in institutional research seem to have an affinity for working with computers.

Addressing each of the questions highlighted in this chapter should help the institutional researcher decide whether participating in an inter-institutional data exchange is in the best interest of her or his institution.

References

Brinkman, P. T. (ed.). *Conducting Interinstitutional Comparisons.* New Directions for Institutional Research, no. 53. San Francisco: Jossey-Bass, 1987.

Brinkman, P. T., and Krakower, J. *Comparative Data for Administrators in Higher Education.* Boulder, Colo.: National Center for Higher Education Management Systems, 1983.

Brinkman, P. T., and Teeter, D. J. "Methods for Selecting Comparison Groups." In P. T. Brinkman (ed.), *Conducting Interinstitutional Comparisons.* New Directions for Institutional Research, no. 53. San Francisco: Jossey-Bass, 1987.

Middaugh, M. F. "The Nature and Scope of Institutional Research." In J. B. Presley (ed.), *Organizing Effective Institutional Research Offices.* New Directions for Institutional Research, no. 66. San Francisco: Jossey-Bass, 1990.

Russell, A. B. *Advances in Statewide Higher Education Data Systems.* Denver, Colo.: State Higher Education Executive Officers, 1995.

Russell, A. B., and Rodriguez, E. M. (eds.). *Compendium of National Data Sources on Higher Education.* Denver, Colo.: State Higher Education Executive Officers, 1993.

Teeter, D. J. "The Politics of Comparing Data with Other Institutions." In J. W. Firnberg and W. F. Lasher (eds.). *The Politics and Pragmatics of Institutional Research.* New Directions for Institutional Research, no. 38. San Francisco: Jossey-Bass, 1983.

Teeter, D. J., and Brinkman, P. T. "Peer Institutions." In M. A. Whiteley, J. D. Porter, and R. H. Fenske (eds.). *The Primer for Institutional Research.* Tallahassee, Fla.: The Association for Institutional Research, 1992.

Teeter, D. J., and Christal, M. E. "Establishing Peer Groups: A Comparison of Methodologies." *Planning for Higher Education,* 1987, 15 (2), 8–17.

Terenzini, P. T., Hartmark, L., Lorang, W. G., Jr., and Shirley, R. C. "A Conceptual and Methodological Approach to the Identification of Peer Institutions." *Research in Higher Education,* 1980, 12 (4), 347–364.

JAMES F. TRAINER is director of the Higher Education Data Sharing Consortium located on the campus of Franklin and Marshall College in Lancaster, Pennsylvania.

A variety of technological resources are available to facilitate data sharing. This appendix highlights a number of software programs and Internet addresses that should prove useful in helping researchers enhance their data-sharing capabilities.

Appendix A: A Computer and Network Resource Guide to Support Data Sharing

James C. Fergerson

The Internet is an arena that is changing so rapidly that much of what is written for the printed media will be out of date by the time the text reaches its audience. Six months of technical changes on the World Wide Web are like a decade of change in most industries. However, an attempt has been made to bring together pointers to some of the more useful (and stable) links available to institutional researchers. All of the Uniform Resource Locator (URL) references cited here are available as links through the World Wide Web. All listed links were active at the time this appendix went to press, but be aware that Internet links frequently change or move unpredictably. In fact, it is almost a rule of thumb that the more popular a site becomes, and the more it is developed, the more likely it is that the link will change. If you should come across a link that has moved, the authors will usually provide a forwarding link to the new location. Sometimes entering a partial URL path name will take you up to a level where more information is available. You can also search for a link using a keyword search engine such as Digital's Alta Vista (URL: http://altavista.digital.com/). Programs and links are listed alphabetically within categories and include author names, page titles, and URL references where appropriate. Finally, institutional researchers should be aware and make grateful use of the extensive Internet Resources for Institutional Researchers Web page being compiled by John H. Milam, Jr. of George Mason University (URL: http://apollo.gmu.edu/~jmilam/air95.html). This is indeed an excellent resource that will continue to grow and improve, whereas printed guides such as this are doomed to slowly decay upon shelves. (Note: URLs may have been split between lines in printing, and some may end with a period because of their position in the text. They must be entered as a single line in a WWW browser. Do not include line-splitting hyphens or terminal periods.)

Glossary of Program Titles and Internet Addresses Cited in Chapter Five

Adobe Acrobat .pdf file reader freeware is available for a variety of computers at URL: http://www.adobe.com/Acrobat/readstep.html. Writing files, however, requires the use of the commercial software. Adobe also provides plug-ins to view .pdf files through Netscape.

Anarchie is a File Transfer Protocol (FTP) client for Macintosh computers with a TCP/IP network connection. The product eliminates the need to learn the FTP command set, and all necessary translations and conversions are done by the software. Downloaded files appear on the desktop computer fully converted and ready to use. Anarchie can be found at: ftp://sumex-aim.stanford.edu/info-mac/comm/tcp/anarchie-16.hqx. (Check for newer versions. Filenames may differ slightly at different mirror sites.)

BrowserWatch Page by Dave Garaffa is a reference collection with news and information about all major browsers, pointers to software, new releases, etc. It is available at URL: http://www.browserwatch.com/.

Cgiemail WWW "forms processing" software information is available at: URL: http://web.mit.edu/afs/athena.mit.edu/astaff/project/wwwdev/www/dist/mit-dcns-cgi.html.

Charm Net Personal IP Page and other information about getting connected to the Internet via SLIP/PPP or other means are available at URL: http://www.charm.net/pip.html. Most commercial Internet service providers supply new users with the required software, along with installation support. A number of Internet Starter Kits are available at anonymous FTP software sites or through computer stores.

Common Gateway Interface Page is available at URL: http://hoohoo.ncsa.uiuc.edu/cgi/overview.

CompuServe Home Page and WorldsAway *avatars* information is available at URL: http://www.compuserve.com/prod_services/consumer/cis/cis.html.

CReAte Your Own Newspaper (CRAYON) information is available at URL: http://crayon.net/.

CU-SeeMe: Frequently Asked Questions (by Peter Hein) CU-SeeMe video conferencing information is available at URL: http://pogo.wright.edu/cuseeme/cuseeme.html.

Eudora is a popular electronic mail package available from QUALCOMM Enterprise Software Technologies. Commercial and freely-distributable versions are available for Macintosh and Windows. Information is available at URL: http://www.qualcomm.com/quest/.

Fetch is an FTP client for Macintosh computers with a TCP/IP network connection. The product eliminates the need to learn the FTP command set, and all necessary translations, conversions, etc. are done by the software. Files downloaded through Fetch appear on the desktop computer fully converted and ready to use. Fetch can be obtained by anonymous FTP at any of the info-mac software archive mirrors in the comm/tcp/ directory. The path to the main (but often busy) archive is ftp://sumex-aim.stanford.edu/info-mac/comm/tcp/fetch-301.hqx.

Gopher clients and servers for many computers are available at URL: gopher://boombox.micro.umn.edu:70/11/gopher. Among the more popular clients are: TurboGopher or MacGopher (for Mac) and WinGopher or The Gopher Book (for Windows). (Web browsers will also display Gopher sites, so special Gopher software may not be needed.)

Gopher: Frequently Asked Questions by Paul Lindner provides a general introduction to Gopher and pointers to software and documentation. It is available at URL: gopher://mudhoney.micro.umn.edu:70/00/Gopher.FAQ.

ListProc is a popular mailing list manager that may be licensed without charge by institutions which are members of the Corporation for Research and Educational Networking (CREN). See URL: http://www.cren.net/www/listproc/listproc.html for details. Some assistance from a system administrator will be required to install the software and to do the initial setup for mailing lists.

Lynx is the most popular Web browser for persons who have text-only access to the Internet. It is a mainframe-based program. The *Lynx User's Guide* can be found at URL: http://www.cc.ukans.edu/lynx_help/Lynx_users_guide.html.

Majordomo: Frequently Asked Questions (FAQ) by David Barr is available at URL: http://www.math.psu.edu/barr/majordomo-faq.html.

Microsoft Internet Explorer is Microsoft's free Web browser. (Microsoft and Netscape are engaged in a serious battle to win market share.) URL: http://www.microsoft.com/ie/go/reajp4.htm.

Mosaic, developed by the National Center for Supercomputing Applications, was the application which caused interest in the WWW to explode. See URL: http://www.ncsa.uiuc.edu/SDG/Software/ for the pointers to Mosaic releases information for various platforms.

Netphone information and demonstration software can be found at URL: http://www.emagic.com/netphone/mainblurb.html.

Netscape is replacing Mosaic as the most popular Web browser. *Welcome to Netscape* can be found at URL: http://home.mcom.com/.

Personal Internet Access Using SLIP or PPP: How You Use It, How it Works by Frank Hecker is available at URL: ftp://ftp.digex.net/pub/access/hecker/internet/slip-ppp.txt. Information on The Internet Adaptor (TIA), a commercial product that allows people without access to a SLIP or PPP server to use similar features from a standard Unix log-in account, is available at URL http://marketplace.com/tia/.

RealAudio Player information and freeware are available at URL: http://www.realaudio.com/. RealAudio is a product of Progressive Networks, Inc.

Standard Survey Responses developed by the University of California, Berkeley and the University of California, Irvine are available on the Web.
Berkeley survey URL:
http://cois.chance.berkeley.edu/planning/IC/Stand.Surv.RPT.html.
Irvine survey URL: http://www.oasim.uci.edu/~oas/ssr/.

University of Arizona Data and Planning Support Office can be reached at URL: http://www.oir.arizona.edu/.

Wide Area Information Server (WAIS) information is available through comp.infosystems.wais FAQ at URL: http://www.cis.ohio-state.edu/hypertext/faq/usenet/wais-faq/getting-started/faq.html.

World Wide Web: Frequently Asked Questions by Thomas Boutell and Boutell.Com, Inc. is available at URL: http://www.boutell.com/faq/.

General World Wide Web and HTML References and Tutorials

Tim Berners-Lee. *How to Put Your Data on the Web.* CERN.
URL: http://www.w3.org/hypertext/WWW/Provider/Overview.html

Tim Berners-Lee. *Style Guide for Online Hypertext.* CERN.
URL: http://www.w3.org/hypertext/WWW/Provider/Style/Overview.html

Tim Berners-Lee. *Tools for WWW Providers.* CERN.
URL: http://www.w3.org/hypertext/WWW/Tools/Overview.html

Tim Berners-Lee. *Web Etiquette.* CERN.
URL: http://www.w3.org/hypertext/WWW/Provider/Etiquette.html

Ian Graham. *Introduction to HTML.*
URL: http://www.utirc.utoronto.ca/HTMLdocs/NewHTML/htmlindex.html

Ian Graham. *Bibliography of HTML Reference Documents.*
URL:http://www.utirc.utoronto.ca/HTMLdocs/NewHTML/bibliography.html

Kevin Hughes. *Entering the World-Wide Web: A Guide to Cyberspace Enterprise Integration Technologies.* May 1994.
URL: http://www.eit.com/web/www.guide/

Kevin Hughes. *From Webspace to Cyberspace.* Enterprise Integration Technologies, 1995.
URL: http://www.eit.com:80/creations/papers/
(available as Adobe .pdf file)

Nelson Laviolette. *The Web Designer.*
URL: http://www.kosone.com/people/nelson/nl.htm

National Center for Supercomputing Applications. *A Beginner's Guide to HTML.*
URL: http://www.ncsa.uiuc.edu/General/Internet/WWW/HTMLPrimer.html

National Center for Supercomputing Applications. *Starting Points for Internet Exploration.*
URL: http://www.ncsa.uiuc.edu/SDG/Software/Mosaic/StartingPoints/NetworkStartingPoints.html

Alan Richmond. *The Web Developer's Virtual Library.* An award-winning resource guide to introductory and advanced Web usage, with extensive technical developer's information.
URL: http://WWW.Stars.com/Tutorial/

SingNet. *WWW and HTML Developer's JumpStation.*
URL: http://oneworld.wa.com/htmldev/devpage/dev-page.html

James "Eric" Tilton. *Composing Good HTML.* December 1995.
URL: http://www.cs.cmu.edu/~tilt/cgh/

Educational Collections in General Internet Subject Catalogs

These subject catalogs provide a quick reference to almost any topic. They are a good place to begin any Internet search.

Alta Vista. Digital Equipment Corporation. Alta Vista is not a subject guide, but it is perhaps the most extensive Internet search engine available. Virtually anything can be found using simple or Boolean keyword searches.
URL: http://altavista.digital.com/

Clearinghouse for Subject-Oriented Internet Resource Guides. University of Michigan, Internet Resource Discovery Project.
URL: http://www.lib.umich.edu/chhome.html

EINet Galaxy. Education links collection.
URL: http://galaxy.einet.net/galaxy/Social-Sciences/Education.html

Lycos Catalog of the Internet.
URL: http://a2z.lycos.com/Education/

The Whole Internet Catalog. Global Network Navigator, O'Reilly and Associates.
URL: http://webcrawler.com/select/ed.new.html

World-Wide Virtual Library.
URL: http://www.csu.edu.au/education/library.html

Yahoo!
URL: http://www.yahoo.com/Education/

Other Educational Links of Interest

Chronicle of Higher Education. Academe This Week. The public site contains *Events in Higher Education, Chronicle* job postings, and some basic statistics from the annual *Almanac* issue.
URL: http://chronicle.merit.edu/

Chronicle of Higher Education. Academe Today. This is the private Internet edition of the *Chronicle,* containing text of articles from back and current issues, on-line versions of published data tables, and much more. The service is password protected, but free to *Chronicle* subscribers.

The Cisco Educational Archive.
URL: http://www.cisco.com/cisco/edu-arch.html

The College Board. College Board newsletters; virtual electronic communities or archives of selected mailing lists; extensive collection of pointers to educational resources.
URL: http://hub.terc.edu/ra/collegeboard.html

CRESST. The National Center for Research on Evaluation, Standards, and Student Testing is a site oriented largely toward K-12 education.
URL: http://www.cse.ucla.edu/CRESSTHome.html

Mike Conlon. *American Universities.* List of pointers to universities and colleges in the United States.
URL: http://www.clas.ufl.edu/CLAS/american-universities.html

Christina DeMello. *College and University Home Pages—Alphabetical Listing.* Comprehensive list of pointers to United States and international colleges and universities.
URL: http://www.mit.edu:8001/people/cdemello/univ.html

Diane K. Kovacs. *Directory of Scholarly E-conferences.* Directory of over 1700 electronic discussion groups, organized by topic and searchable by keyword.
URL: http://www.austin.unimelb.edu.au:800/1s/acad

Educational Policy Analysis Archives. EPAA is a peer-reviewed electronic journal published at the College of Education at Arizona State University.
URL: http://seamonkey.ed.asu.edu/epaa/

Educational Resources Information Center (ERIC). *AskERIC Virtual Library.*
URL: http://ericir.syr.edu/

Educational Resources Information Center (ERIC). *ERIC Database Search.*
URL: http://ericir.syr.edu/Eric/

HEPROC. *Higher Education Resources and Assistance.*
http://www.digimark.net/educ

Magpie Internet Education Resources Collection.
URL: http://www.aber.ac.uk/~magwww/index_ht1.html

James J. O'Donnell. *New Tools for Teaching Page.*
URL: http://ccat.sas.upenn.edu/teachdemo

Peterson's Guides Inc. *Peterson's Education Center.* Contains pointers to colleges and universities, with emphasis on needs of applicants. Colleges participating in the Common Application Form consortium will find a downloadable software version of the form linked to their page.
URL: http://www.petersons.com/

The Princeton Review. Results of Princeton review survey of admissions offices and students; Princeton Review's controversial top 20 lists.
URL: http://www.review.com/

Rand's Institution on Education and Training.
URL: gopher://info.rand.org:70/11/IET/

U.S. News On-line. *School Rankings.* The 1996 *U.S. News & World Report* college rankings.
URL: http://www.usnews.com/usnews/fair/RNK_MAIN.HTM

Useful Government Sites

New York State Education Department. *New York State Degree-granting Institution Profiles.* Longitudinal files compiled from many years of New York state institutions' IPEDS and state data submissions. Contains New York institutions only, but it is a useful reference.
URL: gopher://unix5.nysed.gov:70/11/Higher%20Education/NYS%20Degree-Granting%20Institution%20Profiles

U.S. Bureau of the Census. *1990 U.S. Census LOOKUP.* Form-driven interactive browsing of 1990 Census data.
URL: http://www.census.gov/cdrom/lookup

U.S. Bureau of the Census. *Uncle Sam's Reference Shelf.* Contains the 1995 *Statistical Abstract of the United States.*
URL: http://www.census.gov:80/stat_abstract/

U.S. Department of Education.
URL: http://www.ed.gov/

U.S. Department of Education. Public IPEDS data series. Contains most recently available IPEDS data. Files are *large*.
URL: gopher://gopher.ed.gov:10000/11/data/postsec/ipeds

Institutional Research Offices and Resources

The list below contains some representative examples of colleges, universities, and institutional research organizations with home pages or factbooks. It is not intended to be exhaustive. The number of institutional research offices with home pages has nearly tripled in six months. See John Milam's collection of institutional research home pages and Todd Massa's collection of electronic factbooks to track the latest additions to the Internet.

Todd R. Massa. *The Electronic Factbook Clearinghouse.* This is an up-to-date collection of electronic factbooks published by institutional research offices. A section on resources and strategies for building electronic factbooks is also available.
URL: http://www.willamette.edu/~tmassa/factbooks

John H. Milam, Jr. *Internet Resources for Institutional Research.* This is THE all-out, award-winning, most comprehensive and up-to-date on-line collection of links related to institutional research issues. A sub-page contains a list of nearly 100 institutional research offices with home pages.
Resources URL: http://apollo.gmu.edu/~jmilam/air95.html
IR Offices with home pages:
URL: http://apollo.gmu.edu/~jmilam/air95/offices.html

Association for Institutional Research.
URL: http://www.fsu.edu/~air/home.htm

Bates College.
URL: http://www.bates.edu/IR/IR.html

Canadian Institutional Researchers and Planners Association.
URL: http://www.usask.ca/cirpa/

Colorado State University (Budget and Analysis).
URL: http://www.colostate.edu/Depts/OBIA/obia.html

Georgia State University (Gopher).
URL: gopher://gopher.gsu.edu/11/.InstRes/

Rhodes College.
URL: http://www.uta.edu/IRandP/homepage.html

Sante Fe Community College. Office of Institutional Research and Planning.
URL: http://198.78.64.26/itp/ir/irmain.html

Seattle Pacific University. Office of Institutional Research.
URL: http://paul.spu.edu/oir/

Texas Association for Institutional Research.
URL: http://www.uta.edu/IRandP/tair/tairhome.html

University of Arizona. Office of Decision Planning and Support.
URL: http://www.oir.arizona.edu/

University of Ottawa.
URL: http://www.uottawa.ca/~pmercier/main_menu.html

University of Texas at Arlington. Office of Institutional Research and Planning.
URL: http://www.uta.edu/IRandP/homepage.htm

Wake Forest University. Office of Institutional Research.
URL: http://www.wfu.edu/Administrative-offices/Institutional-Research/

Willamette University.
URL: http://www.willamette.edu/ir/index.html

Emerging Technologies That Offer Promise for the Future of Data Sharing

Some of these technologies are still fairly primitive and may not be widely known outside of the technical community. Others are in wide use, but their potential as tools for encouraging dialog and data exchange in institutional research may not be recognized.

David Barr. *Majordomo: Frequently Asked Questions (FAQ).* Information about the Majordomo mailing list software.
URL: http://www.math.psu.edu/barr/majordomo-faq.html

Jeff Boulter and Dave Maher. *CRAYON—CReAte Your Own Newspaper.* CRAYON uses Web forms to allow you to design a personalized daily newspaper containing only the news items you are interested in. The concept could be adapted to collect customized updates for institutional researchers, collected on demand from many educational data sites.
URL: http://crayon.net/

CU-SeeMe Home Page. Desktop videoconferencing software from Cornell University for Macintosh and PC. Transmits sound and limited video.
URL: http://magneto.csc.ncsu.edu/Multimedia/Classes/Spring94/projects/proj6/cu-seeme.html

Paul Grant. *IRC for the Newcomer.* WWW page. Internet Relay Chat (IRC) software offers text-based real-time interactive teleconferencing on "channels". It is perhaps the Internet equivalent of the citizens' band radio. While IRC is primarily used for social purposes, it could be used for committee conferences and special interest discussions.
URL: http://irc.ucdavis.edu/undernet/underfaq/index.html

Helen Trillian Rose. *Internet Relay Chat FAQ.*
URL: http://www.kei.com/irc.html

Netphone Home Page. Netphone is commercial software that allows users to place real-time calls over the Internet using a microphone and a 14.4K baud modem. Long distance carriers are bypassed if both parties have the software.
URL: http://www.emagic.com/

Progressive Networks. *RealAudio Home Page*.
Software for recording and transmitting real-time audio over the Internet. Professional conference presentations could be taped and broadcast to a wider community from a RealAudio server.
URL: http://www.realaudio.com/

Sun Microsystems, Inc. *Java™: Programming for the Internet*. Sun's Java™ programming environment only became available as this went to press, but Java and related applications are already beginning to be common on the Internet. Java programs include applications and mini-applications (*applets*) that can be automatically downloaded from the Internet on an as-needed basis and that will function on multiple operating systems. The portability and modular object-oriented nature of Java makes it an ideal platform for expanding and developing Web-based pages beyond simple hypertext and graphics. With Java, Web pages can include real-time animations, complex interactive end-user programs, and so forth. Java capabilities have been built into the latest versions of some Web browsers. Expect to see much more about Java in the future, but until then, find out more at URL: http://java.sun.com/allabout.html.

Wide Area Information Server (WAIS). WAIS software searches large text archives and returns documents that match certain keywords. WAIS servers can be configured to periodically check for new matches. A collection of pointers to WAIS software for various operating systems can be found at URL: http://www.cis.ohio-state.edu/hypertext/faq/usenet/wais-faq/getting-started/faq.html.

Virtual Reality Modeling Language (VRML). *The Web Gate to Virtual Reality*. A collection of works about the present and future of 3-dimensional navigation of the Internet.
URL: http://Web.Actwin.Com:80/NewType/vr/vrml/index.htm

Ari Luotonen and Tim Berners-Lee. *WIT-World Wide Web Interactive Talk Page*. One example of a forms-based WWW discussion format designed to encourage interactive and progressive mail-based debates and to carry them to conclusion without the mayhem and repetition that commonly occurs in USENET newsgroups. Anyone can propose discussion on a specific topic or proposal, and the archived discussions are available to all.
URL: http://www.w3.org/hypertext/WWW/Discussion

JAMES C. FERGERSON is director of institutional research at Bates College in Lewiston, Maine. He can be reached over the Internet at his IR home page at URL: http://www.bates.edu/IR/IR.html.

This appendix should serve as an important reference for researchers seeking to learn more about data-sharing opportunities. Many of the organizations listed here can serve as models for those interested in creating their own data-sharing endeavors.

Appendix B: Data-Sharing Organizations, Resources, and Opportunities

James F. Trainer

The chapters in the main body of this volume provide much information about the formation, organization, and function of inter-institutional data exchanges. Among other things, they provide a typology for identifying and understanding data-sharing opportunities and organizations. Following is a compilation of information on numerous data-exchange organizations. The list is subdivided into four categories: 1) organizations whose primary or secondary function includes comprehensive data exchange; 2) opportunities to share data for specific limited purposes; 3) resources to assist institutions in gathering comparative information; and 4) a list of sample data-sharing presentations titles from the Association for Institutional Research's 35th Annual Forum, held in Boston in May 1995.

The reader should realize, however, that this list is provided only to highlight examples of data-sharing organizations and opportunities. Unfortunately, the list suffers two weaknesses. First, it is not all-inclusive; many more data-sharing organizations and opportunities exist than could possibly be listed here. Second, many of the groups that are listed have regional, functional, or invitational restrictions on membership. Nonetheless, even those with closed memberships can serve as models for individuals and institutions interested in

---

I am indebted to Carole M. Koza and Elizabeth M. McCalmont, students at Franklin and Marshall College and employees of the Higher Education Data Sharing Consortium, who assisted in the compilation of the information included in this appendix.

perhaps joining one or another of these groups or initiating their own data-sharing organizations or informal activities.

Sample Data-Sharing Organizations

Association of American Universities Data Exchange (AAUDE)
Gary A. Rice
Director
Institutional Studies
University of Washington
172 Administration Building
Box 351263
Seattle, WA 98195
(206) 616–7440
E-mail: grice@u.washington.edu

The AAUDE collects and distributes various annual data sets, including information on institutional enrollments, finances, and faculty, among other topics. While maintaining no official tie with the Association of American Universities (AAU), only AAU institutions are AAUDE members. The Exchange also coordinates special studies from time to time for both public and private AAU institutions.

Association of Catholic Colleges and Universities (ACCU)
One Dupont Circle, NW, Suite 650
Washington, DC 20036
(202) 457–0650

ACCU provides opportunities for its members to receive reports based on the Cooperative Institutional Research Program's (CIRP) freshmen survey and various senior surveys offered by other organizations.

Association of Independent Colleges and Universities in Massachusetts (AICUM)
Clare M. Cotton
President
11 Beacon Street, Suite 1224
Boston, MA 02108–3093
(617) 742–5147
E-mail: aicum@bcvms.bc.edu

AICUM conducts numerous annual studies. These efforts include work on tuition and fees, degree completions, fall enrollments, and student financial aid, among other topics. Similar studies are conducted by various statewide associations all across the country. Readers particularly interested in studies conducted by independent college and university associations should refer to the State-National Information Network/National Institute of Independent Colleges and Universities report cited elsewhere in this appendix.

Coalition for Christian Colleges & Universities (CCCU)
Karen Longman
Vice President for Professional Development Programs
329 Eighth Street, NE
Washington, DC 20002
(202) 546-8713
E-mail: kal@cccu.org

The Coalition for Christian Colleges and Universities conducts a number of regular annual data-sharing activities and surveys on behalf of its membership. These surveys include information on admissions, compensation, enrollment, and tuition and fees. The Coalition received a Fund for Improving Postsecondary Education (FIPSE) grant in 1994 to conduct a study entitled "Taking Values Seriously: Assessing the Mission of Church Related Higher Education." At the heart of this study are a series of comparative data-sharing activities based on nationally-normed surveys such as the Cooperative Institutional Research Program's (CIRP) freshmen survey as well as instruments designed specifically for this project. Although CCCU received funding for three years, the participating colleges have agreed to continue the project for six years to track the 1994 freshmen (10,500) through their senior year and then as alumni two years after graduation. Twenty CCCU members are a part of the FIPSE funded effort, while approximately another thirty institutions participate in the Coalition's overall Collaborative Assessment project.

College Information Systems Association (CISA)
E. Raymond Hackett
Executive Director
Auburn University
4032 Haley Center
Auburn, AL 36849
(334) 844-3082
E-mail: hackera@mail.auburn.edu

CISA assists member institutions in planning and institutional research by assembling and sharing a mutually agreed upon and regularly updated set of information. The CISA membership consists of forty-two independent colleges and universities. Most CISA members are Baccalaureate II Colleges within the Carnegie Classification scheme, and are generally located in the southeastern states with other institutions welcome. CISA provides a useful service in that accurate comparative information is not readily available for many independent colleges, and it is difficult to collect and maintain, especially at institutions with relatively small staffs. In addition to providing comparative information, the CISA staff can assist members in the preparation of their annual institutional factbooks. Beginning with the incoming class of Fall 1996, CISA member institutions will begin a comprehensive student assessment program for the liberal arts institutions, following students from matriculation through alumni status.

Committee on Institutional Cooperation (CIC) Data Exchange
Roger G. Clark
Director
302 E. John Street, Suite 1705
Champaign, IL 61820–5698
(217) 333–8475
E-mail: rgc@uiuc.edu

The Committee on Institutional Cooperation (CIC) is the academic consortium of the eleven Big Ten universities and the University of Chicago. The CIC Data Exchange Panel includes these twelve institutions, plus the University of Illinois, Chicago and the University of Wisconsin, Milwaukee. The panel helps facilitate the data collection and dissemination efforts of the nearly sixty-five CIC panels and groups.

Consortium on Financing Higher Education (COFHE)
Katharine Hanson
Executive Director
238 Main Street, Suite 307
Cambridge, MA 02142
(617) 253–5030

The Consortium on Financing Higher Education (COFHE) has a current membership of thirty-one of the nation's leading private colleges and universities. COFHE conducts annual surveys covering such areas as admissions, financial aid, and tuition and fees. The consortium also directs special studies at the request of the members and coordinates data sharing on freshmen, senior, and alumni surveys. COFHE also monitors and provides policy analysis on federal and independent-sector developments. Membership is by invitation only. COFHE reports are considered proprietary and are generally not available to nonmembers.

Great Lakes Colleges Association (GLCA)
Carol J. Guardo
President
2929 Plymouth Road, Suite 207
Ann Arbor, MI 48105
(313) 761–4833
E-mail: guardo@glca.org

GLCA provides its members with early access to a standard series of publicly available data. Directors of functional areas such as admissions, business, and registration meet annually to share information and to examine issues of common concern.

Higher Education Data Sharing Consortium (HEDS)
James F. Trainer
Director
Franklin and Marshall College
P.O. Box 3003
Lancaster, PA 17604–3003
(717) 399–4448
E-mail: heds@acad.fandm.edu

The Higher Education Data Sharing Consortium (HEDS) is a membership organization of 133 private colleges and universities. It collects and analyzes data for approximately twenty projects a year. These projects include a traditional annual series examining admissions, enrollment, faculty compensation, finance, financial aid, and voluntary support, among other topics. The consortium also conducts analyses of the Cooperative Institutional Research Program's (CIRP) freshmen survey and offers both a senior and alumni survey of its own. (See the listing later in this appendix for additional information on the services offered through CIRP.) The consortium hosts two membership conferences each year. Membership in HEDS is by invitation.

Maryland Community College Research Group (MCCRG)/
Maryland Association of Community Colleges (MACC)
Kimberly Ford
Research Director
Maryland Association of Community Colleges
60 West Street, Suite 200
Annapolis, MD 21401
(410)974-8117

The MCCRG, with representatives of institutional research at all eighteen Maryland community colleges, compiles a data book consisting of forty tables of data concerning enrollment, degrees and certificates awarded, revenues and expenditures, college personnel, and physical facilities. The data book is published annually by the MACC, a college-funded lobbying organization in the state capital, Annapolis.

Metropolitan University Group (MUG)
Theodore Micceri
Coordinator, Institutional Research & Planning
University of South Florida
4202 Fowler Avenue, SVC 5022
Tampa, FL 33620–6990
(813) 974–5513
E-mail: tmicceri@ucs01.cfr.usf.edu

The Metropolitan University Group (MUG) consists of twenty-one metropolitan universities throughout the United States that have agreed to share benchmark data on a regular basis. In order to be a member, a university must be a public university, have a Carnegie Classification of Research I or II or Doctoral I or II, be located in or near a metropolitan area, have a student headcount of at least 15,000, and have a fairly bimodal mix of full-time and part-time students. The group meets as a special interest group at various conferences to discuss their ongoing benchmarking efforts and to work on improvements for succeeding years.

Pennsylvania Independent College and University Research Center (PICURC)
Brian C. Mitchell
Suite 400
800 North Third Street
Harrisburg, PA 17102
(717) 232-8649

PICURC conducts a series of annual studies and reports on undergraduate tuition and fees, admissions, institutional finances, and student financial aid, among other topics. Special PICURC efforts include alumni, faculty, and student surveys. PICURC has conducted studies on higher education participation and access, student retention, and degree completion.

SREB-State Data Exchange
Southern Regional Education Board
Joseph L. Marks
Associate Director, Data Services
592 Tenth Street, NW
Atlanta, GA 30318-5790
(404) 875-9211 x-246
E-mail: joe.marks@sreb.org

The SREB-State Data Exchange compiles comparative data on institutions in fifteen southern states. Data are available both by state and at the institutional level. An annual report is issued and data bases are available on an on-line server.

Southern University Group (SUG)
Marsha K. Moss
Director, Institutional Studies
University of Texas, Austin
202 Main Building, G1100
Austin, TX 78712-1111
(512) 471-3833
E-mail: ismkm@utxdp.dp.utexas.edu

The Southern University Group (SUG) consists primarily of major public universities in the Southern Regional Education Board (SREB) region. With a membership of approximately thirty, SUG provides its institutions the opportunity for informal data exchanges on topics ranging from faculty and students to financial information. Members convene annually to exchange ideas and discuss topics of mutual interest.

Worchester Consortium for Higher Education
37 Fruit Street
Worchester, MA 01609
(508) 754-6829

Each fall the Worchester Consortium for Higher Education collects and shares enrollment data from the colleges and universities in the Worchester area.

Sample Data-Sharing Opportunities

AAUP Annual Faculty Compensation Survey
Ernst Benjamin
Associate General Secretary and Director of Research
1012 Fourteenth Street, NW, Suite 500
Washington, DC 20005
(202) 737-5900
E-mail: ebenjamin@igc.apc.org

The American Association of University Professors (AAUP) Faculty Compensation Survey, the definitive, annual study of faculty salaries, provides comparative full-time faculty salary information based on institutional classification. The survey includes instructional staff data on average salary and tenure appointments by rank and gender, fringe benefit expenditures by rank, and percent increase in salary for continuing faculty.

Arizona Statewide Student Information System
Philip J. Silvers
Senior Assistant to Chancellor, Research & Planning
Pima County Community College District
4905C E. Broadway Street
Tucson, AZ 85709-1270
(520) 748-4745
E-mail: psilvers@pimcc.pima.edu

Over a six-year period, the community colleges and universities in Arizona have produced a statewide student tracking system which is now paying dividends in institutional effectiveness analyses. Through voluntary collaboration, the re-searchers, college presidents, and board members involved in developing this effort have been able to overcome various political, financial, and methodological issues in creating a system that serves colleges, universities, and school systems.

Association of Governing Boards (AGB)
Strategic Analysis Project
Barbara E. Taylor
Vice President, Programs & Research
One Dupont Circle, Suite 400
Washington, DC 20036
(202) 296-8400

AGB has created one of the most comprehensive data bases ever assembled in higher education. The data base contains comparative information on more than fifty key strategic indicators in nine critical decision areas for more than 500 institutions. Boards and administrators can study these data to learn a great deal about where their institutions stand with respect to their peers.

College and University Personnel Association (CUPA)
Higher Education Compensation Benchmarking Surveys
Barbara Wells
Research Associate
CUPA
1233 20th St., NW, Suite 301
Washington, DC 20036
(202) 429-0311 ext. 385

CUPA conducts annual surveys on administrative staff salaries and compensation, faculty salaries by discipline and rank, and chief executive compensation. The first of these efforts includes information on more than 170 administrative positions, the second contains data across five faculty ranks and within 55 disciplines, the final project examines chief executive compensation at more than 900 institutions. In each case, the data are sorted by variables such as institutional control, size, and type as appropriate. A variety of supplemental reports are available for each study.

Consortium for Student Retention Data Exchange (CSRDE)
Theresa Y. Smith
Assistant Provost and Director of Institutional Research
University of Oklahoma
660 Parrington Oval, Room 104
Norman, OK 73019
(405) 325-3681
E-mail: tsmith@uoknor.edu

The CSRDE data exchange was established in August 1994. Currently, CSRDE has 218 member colleges and universities ranging from public to private in control, research to baccalaureate in mission, and highly selective to liberal in admission standards. The consortium has built a national longitudinal retention data base for the general student population and for each of the race and gender subgroups. The 1995–96 data base covers the retention and graduation rates for each of the 1987–94 first-time freshmen cohorts. Each CSRDE distributes a Retention Report to its members summarizing the status of student retention by race, gender, institutional selectivity, and various other institutional characteristics. In addition, a customized report containing benchmark data of a self-selected institutional peer group is prepared for each of the members according to their specifications.

Cooperative Interinstitutional Research Program (CIRP)
Alexander W. Astin
Director
Higher Education Research Institute
UCLA, Graduate School of Education and Information Studies
3005 Moore Hall, mailbox 951521
Los Angeles, CA 90095–1521
(310) 825–1925
E-mail: heri@gse.ucla.edu

The Cooperative Institutional Research Program (CIRP) is an annual national longitudinal study of American higher education. Established in 1966 by the American Council of Education (ACE), CIRP is now the nation's largest and oldest continuing empirical study of American college and university students. Open to all two- and four-year institutions, the CIRP surveys include both an Annual Freshman Survey, which covers demographic, experiential, and attitudinal issues of first-year college students, and a College Student Survey, which can be used in conjunction with the Freshman survey to provide a longitudinal analysis of student satisfaction and outcomes in various aspects of the college experience. The CIRP surveys also include a National Faculty survey administered approximately every four years.

Council for Aid to Education Voluntary Support Survey (CAE)
David Morgan
Vice President for Research
342 Madison Avenue, Suite 1532
New York, NY 10173
(212) 661–5800
E-mail: david_morgan@cae.org

CAE, an independent subsidiary of RAND, conducts an annual Voluntary Support of Education survey that contains data from over 1100 institutions and includes information on general restricted and unrestricted support, current and capital gifts, and giving by source and purpose. The report also includes enrollment, endowment, and E & G expenditure data. CAE offers analytical services aimed at addressing fundraising issues.

Gordon White
Southern Illinois University at Carbondale
Carbondale, IL 62901
(618) 453-2121

National Association of College and University Business Officers (NACUBO)
Benchmarking and Comparative Endowment Studies
James E. Morley, Jr.
President
One Dupont Circle, NW, Suite 500
Washington, DC 20036
(202) 861-2500

NACUBO, an organization with more than 2100 members, conducts a number of annual surveys. The annual Benchmarking Project provides participating institutions with financial statistics and comparative analysis of the administrative and operational costs of approximately 100 colleges and universities. The types of data collected for the report cover a spectrum of topics including accounts payable, departmental costs, admissions figures, costs of hiring a new employee, human resource issues, and purchasing. Overall, the project includes more than 300 individual benchmarks in 40 functional areas. The Comparative Endowment Study annually collects endowment and investment management data from more than 400 colleges and universities.

National Study of Instructional Costs and Productivity
Michael F. Middaugh
Director of Institutional Research & Planning
University of Delaware
325 Hullihen Hall
Newark, DE 19716
(302) 831-2021
E-mail: michael.middaugh@mvs.udel.edu

The National Cost Study is a collaborative effort to collect and analyze data on instructional costs and productivity by academic discipline. With the support of a FIPSE grant, the project is in its third year of data collection in 1995-96. FIPSE's support of this project will continue through 1998. Data in the reports are arrayed by Carnegie institution type with specific institutional identities masked.

Data-Sharing Resources

Academy for Educational Development
Paul T. Bucci
Vice President and Director, Higher Education Management Services
1875 Connecticut Avenue, NW
Washington, DC 20009-1202
(202) 884-8000

Data-Sharing Organizations 101

Computer-Aided Science Policy Analysis and Research (CASPAR)
Fabrizio Golino
Vice President Database Systems
Quantum Research Corporation
7315 Wisconsin Avenue, Suite 631 West
Bethesda, MD 20814
(301) 657-3070
FTP address: ftp.qrc.com

John Minter Associates — National Cooperative Data Share
John Minter
President
2400 Central Avenue, Suite B-2
Boulder, CO 80301
(303) 449-8110

National Center for Higher Education Management Systems (NCHEMS)
Clare Roberts
Publications Manager
P.O. Drawer P
Boulder, CO 80301-9752
(303) 497-0390

National Center for Educational Statistics
Susan G. Broyles
Postsecondary Education Statistics Division
Institutional Studies Branch
555 New Jersey Avenue, NW
Washington, DC 20208-5652
(202) 219-1359

Research Associates of Washington
Kent Halstead
2605 Klingle Road, NW, Box S
Washington, DC 20008
(202) 966-3326

State-National Information Network
Current Research Reports
David Laird and Ken Redd
National Association of Independent Colleges and Universities
1025 Connecticut Avenue, NW
Suite 700
Washington, DC 20036
(202) 785-8866

Sample Data-Sharing Sessions from the Association for Institutional Research's 35th Annual Forum

As the need for comparative data increases, numerous data-sharing opportunities are being developed. Many of these opportunities become projects that result in the production of a variety of papers and reports. The following papers are examples of the type of work that has evolved in this area; each of them was delivered as a part of AIR's 35th Annual Forum.

Benefits and Problems Associated with Data Exchanges

Timothy R. Sanford (moderator), Assistant Provost and Director, Institutional Research, University of North Carolina-Chapel Hill
Marsha Kelman Moss (panelist), Director, Institutional Studies, University of Texas, Austin
Donald J. Reichard (panelist), Associate Vice President, Planning and Institutional Research, University of North Carolina-Greensboro
Mary M. Sapp (panelist), Director, Planning and Institutional Research, University of Miami

Community College-University Collaboration to Better Understand Student Attrition and Retention

William S. Johnson (author), Director, University Evaluation, Arizona State University
Denice Ward Hood (author), Management Research Analyst, Arizona State University
Billie Hughes (author), Coordinator, Phoenix College
Shelly Potts (author), Management Research Analyst, Arizona State University
Marian Gibney (author), Director, Research, Phoenix College

Comparable Standards for Credit Hours

Steven P. Chatman (author), Director, Analytical Studies, University of Missouri System

Comparison of Faculty Salaries with Peer Institutions. Methodology and Elucidation of Results: A Case Study

Usha M. Shivaswamy (author), Assistant Director, Institutional Research, Ball State University
Catherine Palomba (author), Director, Institutional Research and Academic Assessment, Ball State University

Large Scale Data Collection: Implications for Data Exchanges and Reporting

Richard D. Howard (author), Associate Dean, Walsh College of Accountancy and Business Administration
Ernest Payne (author), Institutional Research, University of Arizona

More Timely Departmental Faculty Salary Comparisons

Steven P. Chatman (author), Director, Institutional Research, University of Missouri System

Predicting Graduation Rates: A Study of Land Grant, Research I and AAU Universities

Richard J. Kroc (author), Director, Student Affairs Research, University of Arizona
Dudley B. Woodward (author), Professor, Higher Education, University of Arizona
Richard D. Howard (author), Associate Dean, Walsh College
Patricia S. Hull (author), Senior Research Specialist, University of Arizona

The Retention Status of Underrepresented Minority Students: An Analysis of Survey Results from Sixty-Seven U.S. Colleges and Universities

Theresa Y. Smith (author), Director, Institutional Research, University of Oklahoma, Norman

A Statewide Community College Model for Measuring Faculty Workload

Richard Yankosky (author), Associate Dean, Institutional Services, Frederick Community College
Amy Coveyou (author)
Gohar Farahani (author), Director, Institutional Research and Assessment, Charles County Community College
Jim Darr (author)

A State Plan for Voluntary Exchange of Data on Transfer Students

William W. Hughes (author), Programmer Analyst, University of Alabama
Harriott D. Calhoun (author), Director, Institutional Research, Jefferson State Community College

Using IPEDS Data for Selecting Peer Institutions

John A. Ingram (author), Research Officer, Coordinating Commission for Postsecondary Education, State of Nebraska

What You Can Do With a Statewide Data Base

Jean C. Keating (author), Research and Data Coordinator, Virginia State Council of Higher Education

JAMES F. TRAINER *is the director of the Higher Education Data Sharing Consortium located on the campus of Franklin and Marshall College in Lancaster, Pennsylvania. He is a member of the Association for Institutional Research's Higher Education Data Policy Committee and the National Association of Independent Colleges and Universities' Commission on Policy Analysis.*

INDEX

AAUP Annual Faculty Compensation Survey, 97
Academe, 33
Academy for Educational Development, 101
Accountability: increased call for, 1, 6, 15; inter-institutional data exchange, and, 1; outcomes assessment and, 6
America OnLine, 69
American Association of University Professors (AAUP), 9, 16, 30, 31, 38, 61, 75, 97
Arizona Statewide Student Information System, 97–98
ASCII, 55, 57–58, 64
Association for Institutional Research (AIR), 6, 30, 62, 87, 91
Association of American Universities, 10, 38
Association of American Universities Data Exchange (AAUDE), 9, 10, 38, 92
Association of Catholic Colleges and Universities (ACCU), 92
Association of Independent Colleges and Universities in Massachusetts (AICUM), 92–93
Association of Research Libraries (ARL), 39

Ball State University, 38
Banta, T. W., 6
Bauer, K. W., 15
Benchmarking: defined, 15; in higher education, 6, 15; NACUBO project and, 17; performance, 17; process, 17
Bloom, A. M., 26
Borden, V.M.H., 6
Brinkman, A. M., 26
Brinkman, P. T., 16, 74, 75

Campus Wide Information Systems (CWIS): advantages of, 60; commercial exploitation of, 61–62; data sharing and, 60–66; design questions about, 62–66; design standards for, 64; file storage and, 64; information control/quality and, 60–62; information maintenance and, 64; information ownership and, 63–64; as marketing tool, 60; security/access considerations and, 63; users of, 62–63
Change, 33
Christal, M. E., 16, 18, 75
Chronicle of Higher Education, 33
Coalition for Christian Colleges and Universities (CCCU), 10, 93
College and University Personnel Association (CUPA), 34, 38, 98
College Information Systems Association (CISA), 10, 30, 93–94
Commission of Independent Colleges and Universities of Pennsylvania, 10
Committee on Institutional Cooperation (CIC) Data Exchange, 94
Common Gateway Interface (CGI), 67
CompuServe, 69
Computer Aided Science Policy Analysis and Research (CASPAR), 33, 46, 73, 101
Computers: costs of, 50; micro, 50. *See also* Electronic technologies; Hardware; Software
Consortia, data-sharing: adaptability of, 18; Association of American Universities Data Exchange, 38; characteristics of, 6, 16; comparative data and, 16–19; conferences of, 20; Consortium on Financing Higher Education, 36–37; consulting services and, 21; contact office benefits/drawbacks of, 24–25; cooperation of, 8–9; creating, 11, 45–48; data accuracy and, 17–18; data bases and, 19–21; data collection instruments and, 22–23; data comparison and, 17–18, 23; data confidentiality and, 18–19; data-driven models of, 16; data exchange opportunity and, 45; data security and, 62; data sensitivity and, 24; data-sharing golden rule and, 18; decision making and, 11–12, 44; efficiency and, 21; exchange data and, 47; exchange strategy and, 48; goal setting by, 11; governance of, 11; Great Lakes Colleges Association, 37; ground rules for, 7–12; hardware/software

105

Consortia, data-sharing *(continued)*
considerations and, 49–50; Higher Education Data Sharing Consortium, 35–36; improvement gaps and, 17; institutional benefits of, 16–21; institutional distinctiveness and, 23–24; institutional drawbacks of, 21–24; Internet and, 50–51; IVY-IR, 38–39; key institution data and, 22; listings of, 5, 92–97; membership of, 8, 46–47; Mid-America Conference, 37–38; mission/goals of, 10–11; model making by, 16, 18; monetary costs of, 21; normative data and, 16; origins of, 5; other data sources and, 17; other services of, 20–21; participation of, 9; peer networks/groups and, 19–20, 45–46; policy issues and, 12; product usefulness and, 48; professional development and, 17, 25, 19; report/data-collection design and, 18; report timeliness and, 18; sample listing, 92–97; scope of, 10; skills acquisition and, 24–25; spokespersons for, 12; staff considerations and, 49; sweat equity and, 45; time costs of, 21–22; voluntary nature of, 6, 7–8. *See also by individual organization*

Consortia of Institutions of Higher Education, 5

Consortium for Student Retention Data Exchange (CSRDE), 9, 10, 98–99

Consortium on Financing Higher Education (COFHE), 10, 31, 34, 36–37, 94

Contact office, data-sharing: benefits to, 24–25; costs to, 25; developing, 48–51; doctoral program alignment of, 49; drawbacks for, 25; institutional support of, 25; member institution housing for, 49; professional contacts of, 25; skills acquisition of, 24–25; staff considerations and, 49; time demands on, 25; visibility of, 24

Cooperative associations. *See* Consortia, data-sharing

Cooperative Institutional Research Program (CIRP), 75, 99

Cornell University, 68

Council for Aid to Education (CFAE), 18, 31, 34–35, 75, 99–100

CReAte Your Own Newspaper (CRAYON), 67, 80

Crotty, C., 69

CU-See Me, 68, 81

Data: accessibility, 9, 16–19, 40; accuracy/comparability issues, 17–18, 44; comparative, 6, 16–19, 29, 71–72; comparison issues, 23; confidentiality issues, 7, 18–19, 40; consortium, 17–18; exchange criteria, 47; handling issues, 7; as institutional resource, 29; integrity issues, 7; longitudinal, 17; normative, 16; peer, 17; quality/usefulness issues, 9–10; ratings, 17; sensitivity issues, 24, 40; taxonomy, 16; timeliness issues, 18, 44; use issues, 11–12. *See also* Inter-institutional data sharing

Data base management software (DBMS), 50

Data exchange: data for, 47; within educational community, 33–34; with external organizations, 32–33; with federal agencies, 32–33; forms of, 32–34; ground rules for, 7–12; hardware/software, 40; Internet and, 40, 50–51; intra-/inter-institutional, 33–34; opportunity for, 45; peer group for, 45–46; with the press, 33; product of, 48; with state agencies, 33; strategy for, 48; volume of, 49–50. *See also* Data exchange dimensions; Inter-institutional data sharing

Data exchange dimensions: control of process, 30; formality of arrangements, 30; heterogeneity of participants, 31; media of exchange, 31–32; number of partners, 31; openness, 31; primacy of purpose, 30; provision of analysis, 32; regularity of activity, 30–31; scope of information, 31

Decision making: accurate/timely data and, 44; costs of poor, 42–43; data-sharing associations and, 44–45; decision points and, 41–42; institutional research function and, 29, 42; key questions in, 42; opportunity cost and, 44; reducing uncertainty in, 43; vision and, 44

Dunn, J. A., Jr., 7, 20, 23, 36, 55

Efficiency: comparisons of, 15; data-sharing consortia and, 21; inter-institutional data exchange and, 1, 6

Electronic mail, 58

Electronic technologies: CGI, 67; CRAYON, 67; CWIS, 60–66; electronic mail, 58; GIF, 65; Gopher, 59–60, 63; HTML,

59; interactive forms/scripts, 66–67; Internet, 32, 40, 50–51, 68, 84–89; Lynx, 68; Netscape, 59; personal agents, 67–68; PPP, 68; program listing, 80–82; SLIP, 68; teleconferencing/telepresence, 68; TIA, 68; World Wide Web, 40, 59–60, 63, 82–83. *See also* Computers; Hardware; Software

Enrollment, forecasting, and planning model (EFPM), 54

European Laboratory for Particle Physics (CERN), 59

File transfer protocol (FTP), 20, 32–33, 35–36, 56

Franklin and Marshall College, 56

Fund for the Improvement of Post Secondary Education (FIPSE), 39

Gopher, 59–60, 63, 81

Graphics interchange format (GIF), 65

Great Lakes Colleges Association (GLCA), 37, 94–95

Halstead, K., 45

Hardware, data exchange, 50

Hartmark, L., 16, 75

Higher education: accountability of, 1, 6; benchmarking in, 6, 15; comparative data needs of, 6, 15, 29; complexity of, 41; decision-making in, 29, 41–43; efficiency/effectiveness issues in, 1; inter-institutional practices of, 1, 5; outcomes assessment and, 6; outsourcing and, 44; peer analysis and, 15; performance indicators for, 6; quality movement in, 15, 17

Higher Education Data Sharing Consortium (HEDS), 7–10, 12, 30, 31, 76, 95; automated data sharing, 57; Booth experiment, 54–55; case example, 53–57; data-sharing dimensions, 35–36; file servers, 56–57; FTP, 56; LISTSERV function, 55–56; origins, 35, 53–54; technical problems, 55

Higher Education General Information Survey (HEGIS), 32

Higher Education Publications, Inc., 5

Hoyt, D. P., 16

Hypertext markup language (HTML), 59–60, 65, 82–83

Improvement gaps, 17

Institutional research: comparative data needs and, 15; decision-making support and, 29, 42; inter-institutional peer analysis and, 15; Ivy league schools and, 38–39

Integrated Postsecondary Data System (IPEDS), 11, 15, 18, 31–33, 45, 54, 62, 73–77

Inter-institutional data sharing: accountability and, 1; affiliation and, 10; assessment questions about, 71–77; athletic conference example and, 6–7; benefits of, 16–21, 102; comparative data and, 16–19, 71–72; comparison information and, 73–74; complexity of, 7; contact office benefits/drawbacks of, 24–25; cost issues and, 11; credit hours and, 102; CWIS and, 60–66; data accessibility and, 9, 75–76; data collection and, 22–23; data handling and, 7; data integrity/protection and, 7; data type and, 10; data use and, 11–12; decision making and, 11–12, 29, 44–45; difficulty of, 30; dimensions of, 30–32; do-no-harm rule and, 12; drawbacks of, 21–24, 102; ease of, 9; electronic technologies and, 57–69; faculty salaries/workload and, 102–103; fair play rule and, 12, 18; financial costs and, 76–77; governance issues and, 11; graduate rates and, 103; ground rules for, 7–12; group characteristics and, 6; incentives for, 8–9; increase in, 1, 6, 30; information needs and, 72–73; institutional distinctiveness and, 23; institutional selection and, 74–75; Integrated Postsecondary Data System and, 11; inter-institutional comparison and, 23; key institution data and, 22; large-scale data collection and, 103; linkages of, 10; member cooperation and, 8–9; membership definition and, 9; mission and, 10; opportunities listing, 97–100; organizational goals and, 11; organizations listing, 92–97; origins of, 5; participation in, 8–9; peer institutions and, 104; peer networks and, 19–20; policy issues and, 12; product/service and, 9–10; ratings and, 17; resource issues and, 11; resources listing, 101–102; scope of, 10; sessions listing, 102–104; spokespersons and, 12; statewide data base

Inter-institutional data-sharing *(continued)* and, 104; student retention and, 102–103; technical requirements and, 77; time commitment and, 76; timeliness and, 18; transfer students and, 104; value of, 15; voluntariness of, 7–10. *See also* Consortia, data-sharing; Contact office, data-sharing; Data; Data exchange; Models, data-sharing

Internet, 32, 40, 50–51, 68; address listing (Chapter Five), 80–81; educational collections, 84; educational links, 84–86; emerging technologies listing, 88–89; government sites, 86; institutional research resources, 86–88. *See also* Electronic technologies; World Wide Web (WWW)

Internet Adaptor, The (TIA), 68–69
Internet Relay Chat (IRC), 68
IVY-IR, 38–39

John Minter Associates, 101

Krakower, J., 75

LISTSERV, 20
Lorang, W. G., Jr., 16, 75
Lynx, 68, 81

Maryland Association of Community Colleges (MACC), 95
Maryland Community College Research Group (MCCRG), 95
Massachusetts Institute of Technology (MIT), 38
Metropolitan University Group (MUG), 95–96
Mid-America Conference (MAC), 37–38
Middaugh, M. F., 15, 19, 72
Models, data-sharing: consortial, 18, 34–39; data-driven, 16; data-sharing consortia and, 16, 18; IPEDS prototype and, 11; member goals/mission and, 11; member needs and, 11; nonconsortial, 39; threshold, 16
Money, 6, 33
Montgomery, J. R., 26
Moss, M. K., 21, 23

National Association of College and University Business Officers (NACUBO), 17, 34, 35, 75, 100
National Center for Educational Statistics (NCES), 33, 45, 73–74, 101

National Center for Higher Education Management Systems (NCHEMS), 101
National Cooperative Data Share, 101
National Research Council, 33
National Science Foundation (NSF), 33, 45
National Study of Instructional Costs and Productivity, 39, 100
NetPhone, 68, 82
Netscape, 59, 82
New York Department of Education, 61, 74, 86
Nicklin, J. L., 6
1996 Higher Education Directory, 5

Opportunity cost, 44
Outcomes assessment, 6. *See also* Benchmarking
Outsourcing, 44

Patterson, F., 5
Pearlstein, J., 69
Peer networks: data on, 17; data-sharing consortia and, 19–20; identifying, 45–47
Pennsylvania Independent College and University Research Center, 10, 74
Performance benchmarking, 17. *See also* Benchmarking
Performance indicators, 6, 44
Peterson's Education Center, 61
Point to Point Protocol (PPP), 68–69
Process benchmarking, 17. *See also* Benchmarking
Prodigy, 69

Quality movement, 15, 17

Rawson, T. M., 167
Reichard, D. J., 21, 23
Research Associates of Washington, 101
Rodriguez, E. M., 72, 75
Russell, A. B., 72, 75

Sanford, T. R., 21, 23
Sapp, M. M., 19, 21, 23
Serial Line Internet Protocol (SLIP), 68–69
Shirley, R. C., 16, 75
Software: audio-on-demand, 68; CASPAR, 33, 46, 73; CU-See Me, 68; data exchange, 50; DMBS, 50; EFPM, 54; listing, 80–82; NetPhone, 68; RealAudio, 68; WAIS, 67. *See also by individual listing*
Southern University Group (SUG), 96–97

SREB-State Data Exchange, 96
Stage, F. K., 23
Stanford University, 38
State-National Information Network, 102
Stecklow, S., 17
Strasler, S., 17
Structured query language (SQL), 61
Student-Right-to-Know Act, 18, 68
Sweat equity, 45

Technology. *See* Electronic technologies
Teeter, D. J., 16, 75
Terenzini, P. T., 16, 75
Thomas, C. R., 66
Threshold models, 16
Trusheim, D. W., 15
Tufts-EDUCOM data sharing project, 35, 53

U.S. News & World Report, 6, 17, 33
Uniform Resource Locator (URL), 79
University of California, Irvine, 60
University of Delaware, 39
University of Maryland, 38
University of Minnesota, 59
University of Virginia, 38–39

Whiteley, M. A., 23
Wide Area Information Server (WAIS), 67, 82, 89
Wilson, D. L., 63
Wittstruck, J. R., 18
Worcester Consortium for Higher Education, 97
World Wide Web (WWW), 40, 59–60, 63, 82–83. *See also* Internet
WorldsAway Community Forum, 68

Ordering Information

NEW DIRECTIONS FOR INSTITUTIONAL RESEARCH is a series of paperback books that provides planners and administrators in all types of academic institutions with guidelines in such areas as resource coordination, information analysis, program evaluation, and institutional management. Books in the series are published quarterly in spring, summer, fall, and winter and are available for purchase by subscription as well as by single copy.

SUBSCRIPTIONS for 1996 cost $50.00 for individuals (a savings of 34 percent over single-copy prices) and $72.00 for institutions, agencies, and libraries. Please do not send institutional checks for personal subscriptions. Standing orders are accepted.

SINGLE COPIES cost $19.00 plus shipping (see below) when payment accompanies order. California, New Jersey, New York, and Washington, D.C., residents please include appropriate sales tax. Canadian residents add GST and any local taxes. Billed orders will be charged shipping and handling. No billed shipments to post office boxes. Orders from outside the United States or Canada *must be prepaid* in U.S. dollars or charged to VISA, MasterCard, or American Express.

SHIPPING (SINGLE COPIES ONLY): $10.00 and under, add $2.50; $10.01–$20, add $3.50; $20.01–$50, add $4.50; $50.01–$75, add $5.50; $75.01–$100, add $6.50; $100.01–$150, add $7.50; over $150, add $8.50. Outside of North America, please add $15.00 per book for priority shipment.

DISCOUNTS FOR QUANTITY ORDERS are available. Please write to the address below for information.

ALL ORDERS must include either the name of an individual or an official purchase order number. Please submit your order as follows:
   Subscriptions: specify series and year subscription is to begin
   Single copies: include individual title code (such as IR78)

MAIL ALL ORDERS TO:
   Jossey-Bass Publishers
   350 Sansome Street
   San Francisco, CA 94104-1342

FOR SUBSCRIPTION SALES OUTSIDE OF THE UNITED STATES, CONTACT:
any international subscription agency or Jossey-Bass directly.

OTHER TITLES AVAILABLE IN THE
NEW DIRECTIONS FOR INSTITUTIONAL RESEARCH SERIES
J. Fredericks Volkwein, Editor-in-Chief

IR88	Evaluating and Responding to College Guidebooks and Rankings, *R. Dan Walleri, Marsha K. Moss*
IR87	Student Tracking: New Techniques, New Demands, *Peter T. Ewell*
IR86	Using Academic Program Review, *Robert J. Barak, Lisa A. Mets*
IR85	Preparing for the Information Needs of the Twenty-First Century, *Timothy R. Sanford*
IR84	Providing Useful Information for Deans and Department Chairs, *Mary K. Kinnick*
IR83	Analyzing Faculty Workload, *Jon. F. Wergin*
IR82	Using Performance Indicators to Guide Strategic Decision Making, *Victor M. H. Borden, Trudy W. Banta*
IR81	Studying Diversity in Higher Education, *Daryl G. Smith, Lisa E. Wolf, Thomas Levitan*
IR80	Increasing Graduate Student Retention and Degree Attainment, *Leonard L. Baird*
IR79	Managing with Scarce Resources, *William B. Simpson*
IR78	Pursuit of Quality in Higher Education: Case Studies in Total Quality Management, *Deborah J. Teeter, G. Gregory Lozier*
IR77	Developing Executive Information Systems for Higher Education, *Robert H. Glover, Marsha V. Krotseng*
IR76	Developing Effective Policy Analysis in Higher Education, *Judith I. Gill, Laura Saunders*
IR75	Containing Costs and Improving Productivity in Higher Education, *Carol S. Hollins*
IR74	Monitoring and Assessing Intercollegiate Athletics, *Bruce I. Mallette, Richard D. Howard*
IR73	Ethics and Standards in Institutional Research, *Michael E. Schiltz*
IR72	Using Qualitative Methods in Institutional Research, *David M. Fetterman*
IR71	Total Quality Management in Higher Education, *Lawrence A. Sherr, Deborah J. Teeter*
IR70	Evaluating Student Recruitment and Retention Programs, *Don Hossler*
IR69	Using National Data Bases, *Charles S. Lenth*
IR68	Assessing Academic Climates and Cultures, *William G. Tierney*
IR67	Adapting Strategic Planning to Campus Realities, *Frank A. Schmidtlein, Toby H. Milton*
IR66	Organizing Effective Institutional Research Offices, *Jennifer B. Presley*
IR65	The Effect of Assessment on Minority Student Participation, *Michael T. Nettles*
IR64	Enhancing Information Use in Decision Making, *Peter T. Ewell*
IR61	Planning and Managing Higher Education Facilities, *Harvey H. Kaiser*
IR60	Alumni Research: Methods and Applications, *Gerlinda S. Melchiori*
IR59	Implementing Outcomes Assessment: Promise and Perils, *Trudy W. Banta*
IR58	Applying Statistics in Institutional Research, *Bernard D. Yancey*
IR56	Evaluating Administrative Services and Programs, *Jon F. Wergin, Larry A. Braskamp*
IR55	Managing Information in Higher Education, *E. Michael Staman*
IR47	Assessing Educational Outcomes, *Peter T. Ewell*
IR39	Applying Methods and Techniques of Futures Research, *James L. Morrison, William L. Renfro, Wayne I. Boucher*
IR37	Using Research for Strategic Planning, *Norman P. Uhl*
IR36	Studying Student Attrition, *Ernest T. Pascarella*